From our Kitchen to Yours

Our Best
Blue-Ribbon Recipes

A winning collection of top-notch, delicious recipes

To everyone who enjoys great food without the fuss!

Gooseberry Patch
An imprint of Globe Pequot
64 South Main Street
Essex, CT 06426

www.gooseberrypatch.com
1 800 854 6673

Copyright 2022, Gooseberry Patch
978-1-62093-513-2

....

Do you have a tried & true recipe... tip, craft or memory that you'd like to see featured in a **Gooseberry Patch** cookbook? Visit our website at www.gooseberrypatch.com and follow the easy steps to submit your favorite family recipe.

Or send them to us at:
Gooseberry Patch
PO Box 812
Columbus, OH 43216-0812

Don't forget to include the number of servings your recipe makes, plus your name, address, phone number and email address. If we select your recipe, your name will appear right along with it... and you'll receive a FREE copy of the book!

CONTENTS

Our Best
Blue-Ribbon Recipes

::::::::::::::::::::::::

**First-Class
Shareable Snacks** 6

**Tip-Top
Breakfast & Brunch** 46

**All-Star Soups,
Muffins & Breads** 90

**First-Class Sides,
Salads & Sandwiches** 130

Splendid Savory Suppers 178

Blue-Ribbon Desserts 218

::::::::::::::::::::::::

Index 252

Our Best Blue-Ribbon Recipes

When we hear "blue-ribbon recipes" we start thinking about all of our trips to our state and local county fairs. We think about our very favorite recipes that have been handed down from the best home cooks in our families...mothers, fathers, grandmothers, sisters...even best friends and neighbors. We remember seeing all of those jars of fruits and vegetables, and rows of cakes, pies, cookies and candies lined up to be sampled in the judges' tent at the fair.

Our Best Blue-Ribbon Recipes cookbook is filled with recipes that have not only won blue ribbons, but have also won the hearts of family & friends. Family-favorite recipes like Best-Ever Garlic Cheese Spread (pg. 16) and most-requested recipes like Cheesesteak Egg Rolls (pg. 26) are one-of-a-kind winners in our book. And a great-grandma's French Toast with Praline Sauce (pg. 50), handed down from the late 1800s, is one of those extra-special recipes.

We filled this cookbook with as many of the award-winning, shareable, crowd-pleasing, tried & true recipes we could. From Best-Ever Breakfast Bars (pg. 76) to start the day, to The Best-Ever Potato Salad (pg. 166) and Iowa's Best Corn Chowder (pg. 104) for lunch, to Top-Prize Chicken Casserole (pg. 192) and Best-Ever Lasagna (pg. 204) for dinner, we think you'll find some new family favorites. And no worries...we didn't forget about dessert! You'll want to try Favorite Pecan Pie Cobbler (pg. 228) and Blue-Ribbon Banana Cake (pg. 240), just to name a few.

We hope you enjoy this special recipe collection showcasing the very best from our Gooseberry Patch family & friends. Now let's get cooking!

Cheesesteak Egg Rolls, Page 2

First-Class Shareable Snacks

BLT Bites, Page 40

Chip Chicken Lollipops, Page 24

Jill Burton, Gooseberry Patch

Crunchy Artichoke Fries

A warm veggie treat that everyone loves! Serve with lemon wedges for squeezing over the artichokes.

Makes 4 servings

1/2 c. all-purpose flour
2 eggs, beaten
1 c. panko bread crumbs
salt and pepper to taste
12-oz. jar marinated quartered
   artichoke hearts, drained
1 to 2 T. olive oil

Place flour in a shallow bowl, eggs in a second bowl and panko crumbs in a third; season each bowl with salt and pepper. Pat artichokes dry with paper towels. Coat artichokes in flour; dip into eggs and roll in bread crumbs. Arrange on an ungreased baking sheet; drizzle with olive oil. Bake at 400 degrees for 25 minutes, or until crisp and golden. Serve warm.

Tina George, El Dorado, AR

Fried Dill Pickles

One of our favorite county fair foods! If you've never tried one, what are you waiting for?

Serves 4 to 5

3 eggs
1 c. milk
1 c. Italian-seasoned dry bread
   crumbs
1/4 c. all-purpose flour
15 dill pickle spears, well drained
oil for deep frying
Garnish: ranch or Thousand Island
   salad dressing

Whisk together eggs and milk in a small bowl; mix bread crumbs and flour in a separate small bowl. Dip pickles into egg mixture; roll in crumb mixture to coat. Heat several inches oil to 375 degrees in a deep fryer. Fry pickles 3 to 5 at a time until golden. Drain on paper towels. Serve warm with salad dressing for dipping..

★ HOT TIP ★ For delicious, crispy golden fried pickles, be sure not to crowd the pan...use a large chicken fryer skillet or fry pickles in two batches.

Crunchy Artichoke Fries

Connie Hilty, Pearland, TX

Waffle Fry Nachos

Set the sheet pan right on the table... then just try to keep people away from these cheesy golden fries!

Makes 8 servings

22-oz. pkg. frozen waffle fry
  potatoes
10 slices bacon, crisply cooked and
  crumbled
6-oz. can sliced black olives, drained
2 to 3 tomatoes, diced
3 green onions, sliced
2/3 c. favorite salsa
1-1/2 c. shredded Cheddar cheese
1-1/2 c. shredded Monterey Jack
  cheese
Garnish: sour cream

Arrange frozen potatoes in a single layer on a lightly greased 17"x11" jelly-roll pan. Bake at 450 degrees for 20 to 25 minutes, until crisp and lightly golden. Top with remaining ingredients except sour cream. Return to oven for another 5 minutes, or until cheeses are melted. Serve with sour cream.

Linda McClain, Columbia, NJ

Best Mexican Dip Ever

I've been making this recipe for over 25 years, and have been asked to share it many times over...it's enjoyed by all ages!

Serves 8 to 10

8-oz. pkg. cream cheese, softened
16-oz. can refried beans
15-oz. jar mild, medium or hot salsa
8-oz. pkg. shredded Cheddar cheese
tortilla chips

Spread cream cheese in a lightly greased 9" deep-dish pie plate or 8"x8" baking pan. Spread beans over cream cheese; spoon salsa over beans and sprinkle shredded cheese evenly on top. Bake, uncovered, at 350 degrees for 20 to 25 minutes, until bubbly and cheese is melted. Serve warm with tortilla chips.

★ SOME LIKE IT HOT! ★ Try using extra-spicy salsa and flavored cream cheese for extra zing!

Waffle Fry Nachos

Janie Branstetter, Duncan, OK

Spicy Ranch Party Pretzels

A one-of-a-kind snack mix you just can't get enough of. You may have to double this recipe!

Serves 10 to 12

3/4 c. oil
1-oz. pkg. ranch salad dressing mix
1 T. garlic salt
1 T. lemon pepper
1 T. cayenne pepper
16-oz. pkg. mini pretzel twists or
  thins

Combine all ingredients except pretzels in a large plastic zipping bag; mix well. Add pretzels to bag; shake to coat well. Spread pretzels on an ungreased baking sheet; let stand until dry. Store in an airtight container.

Erin Jones, Smyer, TX

Almond Toffee Popcorn

Movie night will be extra special with a big bowl of this crunchy, nutty popcorn for snacking!

Makes about 12 cups

12 c. popped popcorn
1 c. sugar
1/2 c. butter
1/2 c. light corn syrup
1/4 c. water
1 c. chopped almonds, toasted
1/2 t. vanilla extract

Place popcorn in a large heat-proof bowl; remove any unpopped kernels and set aside. In a large saucepan, combine remaining ingredients except vanilla. Cook over medium-high heat, stirring occasionally, until mixture reaches the soft-crack stage, or 270 to 289 degrees on a candy thermometer. Remove from heat; add vanilla and stir well. Pour over popcorn, mixing until coated. Spread on wax paper to dry.

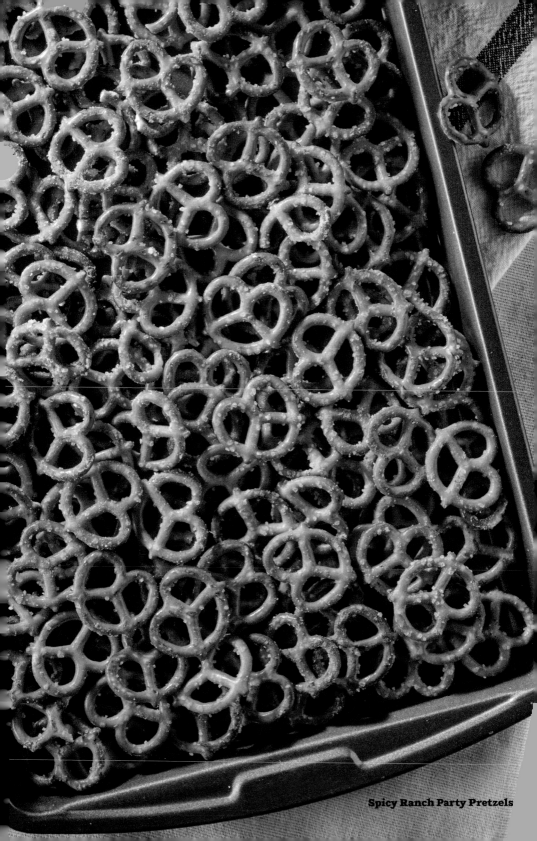

Spicy Ranch Party Pretzels

Cindy VonHentschel, Albuquerque, NM

Jalapeño Cheddar Balls

I made up this recipe one year with some ingredients I had in the pantry and freezer. Now I make these for holiday potlucks and parties. People gobble them up, and I get a lot of really nice feedback.

Makes two dozen

16-oz. pkg. ground pork breakfast sausage
2 to 3 large jalapeño peppers, finely diced and seeds removed
1/2 c. onion, finely diced
1 clove garlic, minced
1/2 c. shredded sharp Cheddar cheese
Optional: chilled jalapeño jelly

In a large bowl, combine all ingredients except optional jelly. Mix well. Using a small cookie scoop, form into one-inch meatballs. Place meatballs on a baking sheet sprayed with non-stick vegetable spray. Bake at 350 degrees for 10 to 15 minutes, until golden. Serve with jalapeño jelly, if desired.

★ DIP IT! ★ Need a cool dip for a spicy appetizer? Sour cream can be mixed with any of the seasoning blends found at the meat counter. Try some different blends for an endless variety of savory dips.

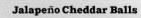
Jalapeño Cheddar Balls

Jenn Erickson, Pacific Grove, CA

Sesame Chicken Tea Sandwiches

These elegant little tea sandwiches are a wonderful addition to a classic tea party, shower or brunch, and even to your child's lunchbox. My daughters love them! It's a wonderful way to use leftover chicken.

Makes 40 mini sandwiches

3 c. cooked chicken, finely chopped
1 c. light mayonnaise, divided
1/4 c. celery, inner stalk and leaves, minced
2 t. sesame oil
1/4 c. sliced almonds
salt and pepper to taste
20 slices soft whole-wheat sandwich bread
1/2 c. toasted sesame seed

In a bowl, combine chicken, 3/4 cup mayonnaise, celery and sesame oil. Crush almonds in your palm and add to bowl; stir to mix. Season with salt and pepper. For each sandwich, place a small scoop of chicken salad on a slice of bread. Top with another slice of bread, press lightly and trim crusts. Cut into 4 triangles on the diagonal. Using a butter knife, spread a thin layer of remaining mayonnaise along the sides of each tea sandwich; dip sandwich into sesame seed to coat mayonnaise.

Valarie Lewis, Clifford Twp., PA

Best-Ever Garlic Cheese Spread

This spread makes a great gift with a loaf of crusty French bread. We've also tried adding it to baked and mashed potatoes...delicious! Butter can be used, but I've found margarine spreads more easily when it's finished.

Makes 15 to 18 slices

1 lb. margarine, softened
3 c. finely shredded Cheddar cheese
1 c. grated Romano cheese
3 T. plus 2 t. lemon juice
2 t. garlic salt or powder
1 t. paprika
1 to 2 t. hot pepper sauce
1/2 t. dry mustard
1/2 t. celery salt
1 loaf French bread, sliced

Combine all ingredients except bread in a large bowl. Beat with an electric mixer on medium speed until well blended. Transfer to a covered container; keep refrigerated. To serve, spread on slices of bread; broil until bubbly and lightly golden.

Sesame Chicken Tea Sandwiches

Lisa Koehler, Oroville, CA

Bacon-Sausage Rye Crisps

We sampled this appetizer at a party years ago and my husband said, "Get the recipe!" I've served it to my family & friends over the years and there is never any left at the end of the evening. Very easy and very yummy!

Makes 10 servings

16-oz. pkg. bacon, crisply cooked and crumbled
16-oz. pkg. hot ground pork sausage, browned and drained
1-1/2 c. shredded Cheddar cheese
1/2 c. mayonnaise
1 loaf party rye bread

In a large bowl, combine cooked bacon and sausage, cheese and mayonnaise. Mix well. Spoon mixture onto rye bread slices and arrange on an ungreased baking sheet. Set oven to broil; set pan on top rack. Watching closely, broil until cheese melts and bread gets crisp around the edges.

Brenda Flowers, Olney, IL

Easy Gumbo Meatballs

After baking, keep these warm in the slow cooker...they're a potluck favorite!

Makes 6 servings

2 lbs. ground beef
4 slices bread, crumbled
3/4 c. evaporated milk
10-3/4 oz. can chicken gumbo soup
10-1/2 oz. can French onion soup

Combine first 3 ingredients; form into one-inch balls. Arrange in an ungreased 13"x9" baking pan; pour soups on top. Bake at 350 degrees for 1-1/2 hours.

★ TOP IT! ★ Chopped olives, tomatoes and sweet onion dress up appetizers in a jiffy, and add loads of flavor.

Bacon-Sausage Rye Crisps

Carla Slajchert, Bellevue, NE

Pepperoni Pizza Braid

This is a recipe I came up with when we wanted something fun for lunch, but didn't want to fuss with making pizza. My kids gobbled it up and declared it a winner! I usually top it with whatever we have on hand. Pepperoni and mushrooms are a favorite combination.

Serves 4 to 6

1 lb. pizza crust dough, thawed if frozen
15-oz. jar pizza sauce, divided
1-1/4 c. shredded mozzarella cheese, divided
18 pepperoni slices
1 t. Italian seasoning
1 T. olive oil
2 T. grated Parmesan cheese

On a floured surface, roll pizza dough into a 13-inch by 7-inch rectangle. Transfer dough to a lightly greased baking sheet. Spread 1/2 cup pizza sauce lengthwise down the center of dough. Sprinkle half of mozzarella cheese over sauce. Layer pepperoni over mozzarella. Sprinkle seasoning over pepperoni; sprinkle with remaining mozzarella. On the long edges of dough, cut slits horizontally all the way to sauce mixture. Lift slits and place over toppings, alternating left and right in a criss-cross style. Drizzle with olive oil; sprinkle with Parmesan cheese. Bake at 400 degrees for 15 to 18 minutes, until golden and cheese is melted. Warm remaining pizza sauce in a small saucepan over low heat; serve with braid for dipping.

★ FLAVOR BOOSTER ★ Use flavored butters to add quick & easy appeal to refrigerated pizza crust. Just mix, melt and brush on crust before baking. Try fresh minced herbs, finely chopped onions or grated Parmesan cheese too.

Pepperoni Pizza Braid

Mary Patenaude, Griswold, CT

Corn Dog Mini Muffins

These make great party appetizers, or serve with soup or salad for a quick lunch.

Makes about 2-1/2 dozen

8-1/2 oz. pkg. corn muffin mix
1 egg, beaten
1/3 c. milk
1 T. honey mustard
4 hot dogs, cut into 1/2-inch pieces
1/2 c. shredded Cheddar cheese

In a large bowl, stir together muffin mix, egg, milk and mustard. Fold in hot dog pieces and cheese. Drop batter by tablespoonfuls into 32 lightly greased mini muffin cups. Bake at 350 degrees for 10 to 15 minutes, until lightly golden. Cool in pan on a wire rack for 5 minutes; turn muffins out of pan.

Barb Bargdill, Gooseberry Patch

Cheesy Tuna Melts

It's the sweet raisin bread and chopped apple that make these sandwiches stand out from all the rest.

Makes 12 servings

1 T. oil
1 c. apple, cored and chopped
3 T. onion, chopped
7-oz. can albacore tuna, drained
1/4 c. chopped walnuts
1/4 c. light mayonnaise
2 t. lemon juice
1/8 t. salt
1/8 t. pepper
6 slices raisin bread, toasted and
    halved diagonally
6 slices sharp Cheddar cheese,
    halved diagonally

Heat oil in a skillet over medium heat; add apple and onion. Cook, stirring occasionally, about 5 minutes, until tender. Remove from heat; transfer to a bowl. Stir in tuna, walnuts, mayonnaise, lemon juice, salt and pepper. Place toast slices on an ungreased baking sheet. Top with tuna mixture and a slice of cheese. Broil 4 to 5 inches from heat for 3 to 4 minutes, or until cheese begins to melt.

Corn Dog Mini Muffins

Barb Rudyk, Alberta, Canada

Chip Chicken Lollipops

This is a fun recipe for a children's party...but even adults love it! I like to experiment with different flavors of seasoned potato chips.

Makes 10 servings

1 egg, beaten
2 T. milk
2 c. potato chips, crushed
4 boneless, skinless chicken
　breasts, cubed
mini wooden skewers
Garnish: favorite dipping sauce

In a shallow bowl, whisk together egg and milk. Spread crushed potato chips in a separate bowl. Dip chicken cubes into egg mixture; coat well with potato chips. Arrange cubes onto a greased baking sheet. Bake at 350 degrees for 10 minutes; turn over. Bake for 10 minutes more, or until golden. Remove baking sheet from oven and insert a skewer into each chicken cube. Serve hot with dipping sauce.

Cinde Shields, Issaquah, WA

Cheesy Spinach-Stuffed Mushrooms

These warm, savory, bite-size beauties always seem to find their way onto my appetizer menu. Everyone loves these little treats!

Makes about 8 servings

10-oz. pkg. frozen chopped spinach,
　thawed and squeezed dry
1/4 c. cream cheese, softened
1 c. crumbled feta cheese
3/4 t. garlic powder
1/4 t. pepper
24 mushrooms, stems removed
1 c. grated Parmesan cheese

In a bowl, combine all ingredients except mushroom caps and Parmesan cheese; mix well. Spoon mixture into mushrooms; place on a rimmed baking sheet. Sprinkle mushrooms with Parmesan cheese. Bake at 350 degrees for about 15 to 20 minutes, until bubbly and heated through. Serve warm.

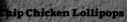
Chip Chicken Lollipops

Melissa Dattoli, Richmond, VA

Cheesesteak Egg Rolls

One of my most-requested party recipes...everyone loves these! They require some prep but once you get the hang of wrapping them, the process goes quickly. Save time by making the filling a day ahead.

Makes 16 to 20

2 c. oil, divided
3/4 lb. deli rare roast beef, thinly sliced and finely chopped
1/2 onion, finely chopped
8 to 10 slices provolone cheese, cut in half
16 to 20 egg roll wrappers

Heat one tablespoon oil in a skillet over medium-high heat; add beef and onion. Cook, stirring occasionally, until beef is browned and onion is tender. Drain on paper towels; let cool for 10 minutes. May refrigerate if preparing ahead of time. To assemble egg rolls: Place an egg roll wrapper in front of you, in a diamond-shape direction. Place a half-slice of cheese horizontally in the center of the diamond; spoon a heaping 1/4 cup of beef filling over cheese. Set out a small glass of water. Gently lift up the bottom corner of wrapper, over the filling. With a moistened finger, dab a little water on the left and right corners of wrapper; fold each side in over the bottom corner. Dab a little water on the top corner; roll up the egg roll gently but firmly. Dab a little more water on the top corner to keep it closed. Repeat with remaining wrappers and filling. To a large skillet, add 1/2 to one inch remaining oil for frying. Heat over medium-high heat. Fry each egg roll for about 4 minutes per side until golden, adjusting heat as needed. Drain egg rolls on paper towels.

★ SNACKS FOR DINNER ★ Why not have appetizers or finger foods for dinner? Set up a family-size sampler with Cheesesteak Egg Rolls, pizza bites, stuffed potato skins and lots of dippers to try too. Don't forget the French fries!

Cheesesteak Egg Rolls

Jill Burton, Gooseberry Patch

Herb-Seasoned Spinach Puffs

Serve with a spicy mustard sauce for dipping.

Serves 8 to 10

2 10-oz. pkgs. frozen chopped
   spinach, thawed
2 c. herb-flavored stuffing mix
1 c. grated Parmesan cheese
6 eggs, lightly beaten
1/3 c. butter, softened

Drain and squeeze spinach to remove all liquid. Combine spinach with remaining ingredients. Mix well and form into 2-inch balls; place on a lightly greased baking sheet. Cover with aluminum foil and refrigerate overnight. Bake at 350 degrees for 15 minutes, or until heated through; remove from baking sheet and cool on paper towels.

Stacie Avner, Delaware, OH

Spiedini

The fresh rosemary really flavors these little sandwiches of grilled cheese...heavenly!

Makes 16 servings

1 loaf French bread, sliced
   1/4-inch thick
2 T. butter, softened
1/4 lb. provolone cheese, sliced
   1/4-inch thick and quartered
16 4-inch sprigs fresh rosemary

Lightly spread 12 slices bread with butter on both sides. Form stacked sandwiches, alternating 3 bread slices with 2 cheese slices. Cut sandwiches into quarters with a serrated knife. Remove leaves from one end of each rosemary sprig; push this end through a quartered sandwich to secure. Repeat with remaining bread, cheese and rosemary sprigs. Arrange on an ungreased aluminum foil-lined baking sheet. Bake at 425 degrees for 4 to 5 minutes, until golden and cheese melts. Serve warm.

Herb-Seasoned Spinach Puffs

Suzanne Erickson, Columbus, OH

Chinese Chicken Wings

Move over, hot wings. These Asian inspired chicken wings are packed with flavor...and they're baked, not fried. Make extra, because the crowd will love them!

Makes 2 to 2-1/2 dozen

2 to 3 lbs. chicken wings, separated
1/2 c. soy sauce
1 c. pineapple juice
1/3 c. brown sugar, packed
1 t. ground ginger
1 t. garlic salt
1/2 t. pepper
Optional: ranch salad dressing,
    celery sticks

Place wings in a large plastic zipping bag; set aside. Combine remaining ingredients except optional garnish. Mix well and pour over wings, turning to coat. Refrigerate overnight, turning several times. Drain wings, discarding marinade; arrange in a single layer on an ungreased jelly-roll pan. Bake at 450 degrees for 25 to 30 minutes, until golden and juices run clear when chicken is pierced with a fork. Serve with ranch dressing and celery sticks, if desired.

Teresa Eller, Kansas City, KS

Best Fry Batter

I have used this tried & true recipe for years. It began with the apple fritters, but now whenever I need a tasty "go-to" appetizer, this is the best!

Makes enough batter for 10 to 12 servings

1 egg
1/4 c. milk
1/2 c. all-purpose flour
1/2 t. baking powder
1/2 t. salt
canola oil for frying
Optional: additional salt to taste

Beat egg in a shallow bowl; stir in milk and set aside. In another bowl, sift together flour, baking powder and salt. Add flour mixture to egg mixture; stir well. In a deep skillet over medium-high heat, bring one to 2 inches canola oil to about 365 degrees. Dip selected foods into batter and coat well; carefully add to hot oil. Fry until golden on both sides and cooked through. Drain on paper towels. Season with salt, if desired.

Variations:

Apple slices: For apple fritters, sprinkle with powdered sugar or roll in cinnamon- sugar.
Onion slices: For onion rings: sprinkle with salt or seasoned salt.
Mushroom caps, zucchini slices: Sprinkle with salt.
Chicken and fish nuggets, shrimp: Cook through; season with salt.

Chinese Chicken Wings

Roseanne Cranston, St. Louis, MO

Texas Caviar

This dip is a hands-down crowd-pleaser. Serve it with your favorite multi-colored tortilla chips.

Makes 4 cups

15-oz. can black beans, drained
   and rinsed
15-oz. can black-eyed peas, drained
   and rinsed
15-1/4 oz. can corn, drained
16-oz. jar salsa
Optional: chopped fresh cilantro

Stir together all ingredients except cilantro; transfer to an airtight container. Refrigerate several hours before serving. Garnish with cilantro, if desired.

Lizzy Burnley, Ankeny, IA

Spicy Hummus

Using canned beans makes this hummus fast and easy to make.

Makes 10 servings

2 c. canned garbanzo beans, rinsed
   and drained
2 cloves garlic, finely minced
1 t. jalapeño pepper, minced
1/2 t. salt
1/2 t. pepper
1 T. lemon juice
1 T. tahini
1 T. olive oil
1/2 to 1 c. tomato juice
Optional: chopped black olives,
   coarsely chopped tomato

Place garbanzo beans in a food processor. Cover and process until blended. Add garlic, jalapeño pepper, salt and pepper. Cover and process until combined. Add lemon juice, tahini and olive oil. Cover and process until well blended. Mixture will be thick. With machine running, slowly add enough tomato juice to make mixture the desired consistency. Transfer to a serving bowl. If desired, garnish with olives and tomato.

Texas Caviar

Robyn Wright, Delaware, OH

Bacon-Wrapped Scallops

Wrapped in bacon strips, these succulent scallops will be snapped up quickly! Be sure to buy sea scallops, which are larger in diameter than the smaller bay scallops.

Makes 22 appetizers

11 slices bacon, cut in half
1/2 c. all-purpose flour
1-1/2 t. paprika
1/2 t. salt
1/2 t white pepper
1/2 t. garlic powder
1 c. milk
1 egg
22 sea scallops
1 to 2 c. panko bread crumbs
Optional: cocktail sauce

In a skillet over medium heat, cook bacon slices for 3 to 4 minutes, until translucent; drain. Combine flour and seasonings in a shallow dish. Beat together milk and egg in a small bowl. Roll scallops in seasoned flour, shaking o excess. Dip scallops in egg mixture, then coat with bread crumbs. Wrap each scallop with bacon and secure with a toothpick. Place scallops on a lightly greased baking sheet. Bake at 400 degrees for about 30 minutes, until bacon is crisp and scallops are cooked through. Serve hot with cocktail sauce, if desired.

Zoe Bennett, Columbia, SC

Tangy Radish Bites

These beautiful little finger sandwiches will be the talk of the party. My friends just love them!

Makes 16 servings

2 T. butter, softened
3 T. fresh chives, chopped
1 T. toasted sesame seed
3/4 t. fresh ginger, peeled and grated
1/4 t. sesame oil
1/8 t. salt
1/8 t. pepper
1 whole-grain baguette, sliced
   1/4-inch thick
10 radishes, thinly sliced
Garnish: edible flowers, pea sprouts

Mix butter, chives, sesame seed, ginger and oil in a bowl. Add salt and pepper and mix well. Spread mixture over one side of each baguette slice. Top with radishes, overlapping slightly. Garnish as desired.

★ SAVE IT! ★ Save bacon drippings for adding flavor to other dishes...it's easy! Just stir in a couple tablespoons of reserved drippings into recipes such as cornbread, scrambled eggs, breakfast potatoes, greens or gravy.

Bacon-Wrapped Scallops

Jen Stout, Blandon, PA

Savory Bacon Bites

We love to make these skewers every year as soon as sweet onions first arrive on produce stands.

Makes 8 servings

**2 sweet onions, each sliced into
    8 wedges**
**8 thick slices hickory-smoked
    bacon, cut in half**
**8 6-inch wooden skewers,
    soaked in water**
2 T. brown sugar, packed
2 T. balsamic vinegar
1 T. molasses

Wrap each onion wedge in a bacon slice. Arrange 2 wedges on each skewer; place in a shallow glass or plastic dish. Combine remaining ingredients; drizzle over skewers. Cover and refrigerate for one hour. Remove skewers from marinade, reserving marinade. Grill, covered, over medium-high heat for 20 minutes, or until onions are crisp-tender, occasionally turning and basting with reserved marinade.

Vicky Dunbar, Fishers, IN

Best-Ever Cheese Spread

This cheese spread really is the best... simplest, too! It was originally made by my grandmother for every holiday gathering. It's so simple to make and is always the first thing requested by the family when I ask, "What can I bring?" I always make extra to send home with those few that just can't get enough of it.

Makes about 4 cups

**4 8-oz. pkgs. cream cheese, room
    temperature**
**4 to 5 T. pasteurized process cheese
    dip**
2 to 3 t. garlic powder
Garnish: paprika
**round buttery crackers or celery
    sticks**

In a large bowl, blend or beat together cream cheese and cheese dip. Stir in 2 teaspoons garlic powder; add more, if desired. (Flavor will intensify as mixture chills.) Spoon mixture into a decorative bowl, smoothing out the top; dust with paprika. Cover and chill. Serve with crackers or celery sticks.

Savory Bacon Bites

Megan Besch, Omaha, NE

Incredible Mini Burger Bites

My family adores these...yours will too! We make them for football parties and summer get-togethers.

Makes 24 mini sandwiches

2 lbs. lean ground beef
1-1/2 oz. pkg. onion soup mix
2 eggs, beaten
1/2 c. dry bread crumbs
3 T. water
1/2 t. garlic salt
1 t. pepper
24 dinner rolls, split
6 slices American cheese, quartered

Garnish: catsup, mustard, shredded lettuce, thinly sliced onion, dill pickles

Mix first 7 ingredients in a bowl; refrigerate for an hour. Spread beef mixture over a greased large baking sheet. Cover with plastic wrap and roll out evenly with a rolling pin. Discard plastic wrap; bake at 400 degrees for 12 minutes. Slice into 24 squares with a pizza cutter. Top each roll with a burger square, a cheese slice and desired garnishes.

★ SIMPLE SWAP ★ Fresh out of hamburger buns? Why not serve burgers on split and toasted English muffins? It's a tasty change from hamburger buns.

Incredible Mini Burger Bites

Deanna Smith, Huntington, WV

BLT Bites

A favorite sandwich becomes an appetizer! Use heirloom tomatoes in different colors for a stunning presentation for a spring buffet.

Makes 10 servings

20 large cherry tomatoes
4 slices bacon, crisply cooked and
    crumbled
1/2 c. light mayonnaise
1/3 c. green onion, chopped
3 T. grated Parmesan cheese
2 T. fresh parsley, finely chopped

Cut a thin slice off the top of each tomato; scoop out and discard pulp. Invert tomatoes onto a paper towel to drain. Combine the remaining ingredients in a small bowl; mix well. Spoon mixture into each tomato; refrigerate for several hours before serving.

Wendy Lee Paffenroth, Pine Island, NY

Market Veggie Triangles

These little triangle sandwiches arrange so nicely on an appetizer tray. Enjoy!

Makes 24 servings

3 cucumbers, chopped
8-oz. pkg. low-fat cream cheese,
    softened
1/4 c. mayonnaise
1 T. lemon juice
1/8 t. hot pepper sauce
1/2 c. red pepper, chopped
1/4 c. onion, finely chopped
1/4 c. green olives with pimentos,
    finely chopped
1 T. fresh parsley, chopped
1/2 t. pepper
12 slices pumpernickel bread, crusts
    trimmed
Garnish: sliced green olives

Place cucumbers in a strainer for 15 to 20 minutes to allow liquid to drain. Combine remaining ingredients except bread and garnish in a bowl. Stir until well blended. Add drained cucumbers; stir again. Refrigerate, covered, for 2 to 3 hours. Slice bread into triangles. Spread with cucumber mixture. Garnish as desired.

BLT Bites

Suzanne Varnes, Palatka, FL

Confetti Cheesecake

A recipe I have made many times... my guests always enjoy it! Serve it with crisp crackers, or slice thinly and serve with a green salad for a light lunch.

Serves 10 to 12

1-1/2 c. round buttery cracker crumbs
1/2 c. butter, melted
2 8-oz. pkgs. cream cheese, softened
2 eggs
1/3 c. all-purpose flour
8-oz. container sour cream
1-1/2 c. green pepper, finely chopped
3/4 c. carrot, peeled and shredded
1/4 c. onion, finely chopped
1/4 t. salt
1/4 t. white pepper
assorted crackers

Combine cracker crumbs and butter; press into an ungreased 9" or 10" springform pan. Bake at 300 degrees for 10 minutes; remove from oven. In a large bowl, beat cream cheese until fluffy; add eggs, one at a time. Stir in flour, mixing well. Add remaining ingredients except crackers, folding vegetables well into batter. Pour into baked crust; bake at 300 degrees for one hour. Turn oven off; cool in oven for one hour before refrigerating. At serving time, remove outer ring of springform pan. Serve with crackers.

★ CRISPY DIPPERS ★ Serve up savory spreads with homemade toast dippers. Use cookie cutters to cut out fun shapes from slices of bread, then brush cut-outs with butter and a sprinkling of herbs. Bake in a 200-degree oven until crisp and golden.

Confetti Cheesecake

Anne Alesauskas, Minocqua, WI

Avocado Feta Dip

My family doesn't care for tomatoes but we love red peppers...so we love this!

Makes 3 cups, serves 12

2 avocados, halved, pitted and diced
3/4 c. crumbled feta cheese
1 red pepper, diced
1 green onion, thinly sliced
1 T. lemon juice
2 t. dill weed
1/4 t. salt
1/4 t. pepper

Combine all ingredients in a serving bowl; mix until well blended.

Della Jones, Georgetown, KY

3-Cheese Artichoke Bites

Mini appetizers filled with Cheddar, Parmesan and mozzarella cheese... scrumptious!

Makes 3-1/2 to 4 dozen.

1 onion, chopped
1 clove garlic, minced
1 T. oil
2 6-1/2 oz. jars marinated artichokes, drained and chopped
6 eggs, beaten
1 c. shredded Cheddar cheese
1 c. shredded mozzarella cheese
1 c. grated Parmesan cheese
1/2 t. Italian seasoning
1/4 c. fresh parsley, chopped
1/4 t. pepper
1/8 t. Worcestershire sauce
1/8 t. hot pepper sauce
1/4 c. Italian-seasoned dry bread crumbs
Optional: additional fresh parsley, chopped

In a skillet over medium heat, sauté onion and garlic in oil until tender; drain and set aside. Combine artichokes, eggs, cheeses, seasonings and sauces in a large bowl; mix well. Stir in onion mixture and bread crumbs. Fill greased mini muffin cups 2/3 full. Bake at 325 degrees for 15 to 20 minutes, until firm and golden. Serve warm, sprinkled with additional parsley, if desired.

Avocado Feta Dip

Dutch Baby with Spiced Fruit, Page 54

CHAPTER TWO

Tip-Top Breakfast & Brunch

Steak & Egg Hash, Page 68

Cream Cheese Danish, Page 88

Barbara Cebula, Chicopee, MA

Gramma's Apple Biscuit Coffee Cake

This is a recipe handed down from my mother to me. It is very tasty with a cup of hot tea or coffee on a chilly day.

Serves 6 to 8

2 T. butter, melted
2 cooking apples, peeled, cored
  and sliced
1/4 c. raisins
8-oz. tube refrigerated biscuits,
  quartered
1/4 c. brown sugar, packed
1/4 c. light corn syrup
1 egg, beaten
1/2 t. cinnamon
Optional: 1/4 c. chopped walnuts
1 T. chilled butter, diced

Spread melted butter in the bottom of a 9" round cake pan. Arrange sliced apples over butter; sprinkle raisins over apples. Arrange biscuit pieces over apples. In a bowl, mix together brown sugar, corn syrup, egg and cinnamon until well blended and brown sugar is dissolved; spoon over biscuits. Sprinkle walnuts over top, if using; dot with chilled butter. Bake at 350 degrees for 25 to 30 minutes. Invert onto a serving plate; spoon sugary juices from pan over top. Cut into wedges and serve.

★ SQUEEZE IT! ★ Sprinkle a little fresh lemon juice over sliced apples before baking...the tart juice will bring out the flavor of the apples.

Gramma's Apple Biscuit Coffee Cake

Vickie Wiseman, Liberty Township, OH

French Toast with Praline Sauce

I can remember making this delicious recipe with my great-grandmother. She taught me that whenever I am using cinnamon, I should add some nutmeg and cardamom to enhance the flavor. I believe this was actually her mother's recipe, from the late 1800s. Grandma always used fresh-baked bread, but any good bread will work.

Makes 12 servings

1 loaf bread, sliced 1-inch thick
6 eggs
1/2 c. whipping cream
1 T. brown sugar, packed
2 t. vanilla extract
1 t. cinnamon
1/2 t. nutmeg
1/4 t. cardamom

Set out bread slices for one to 2 hours to dry. In a large bowl, combine remaining ingredients. Beat with an electric mixer on medium speed until smooth and brown sugar is dissolved. Pour one cup of mixture into a greased 13"x9" baking pan. Arrange bread slices on top; pour remaining egg mixture evenly over bread. Cover and refrigerate overnight. If desired, heat a greased cast-iron skillet or electric griddle. Add bread slices, a few at a time; cook until golden on both sides. (This step adds color to the toast but may be omitted.) Return bread slices to baking pan. Spoon Pecan Praline Syrup over top. Bake at 350 degrees until set and golden, about 30 minutes.

Pecan Praline Syrup:

1 T. butter
3/4 c. brown sugar, packed
1/2 c. pure maple syrup
3/4 c. chopped pecans, toasted

Melt butter in a saucepan over medium heat. Add brown sugar and maple syrup; cook and stir until smooth. Bring mixture to a boil. Reduce heat to low and simmer for one minute, stirring constantly. Stir pecans into syrup.

French Toast with Praline Sauce

Jo Ann, Gooseberry Patch

Cheesy Hashbrown Nuggets

Yum! These are always welcome on a brunch or appetizer buffet. Swap in your favorite cheese, if you like.

Makes about 2 dozen

6 slices bacon
1 egg, beaten
1/2 c. sour cream
salt and pepper to taste
1-1/2 c. shredded sharp Cheddar cheese
20-oz. pkg. frozen shredded hashbrowns, thawed

Cook bacon in a skillet over medium heat until crisp. Drain; set aside bacon on paper towels. In a bowl, whisk together egg, sour cream and seasonings; stir in cheese. Fold in hashbrowns and bacon. Scoop a heaping tablespoon of hashbrown mixture and make a ball. Add mixture to well-greased mini muffin cups by heaping tablespoonfuls. Bake at 425 degrees for 20 minutes, or until hot and golden. Serve warm.

Nola Coons, Gooseberry Patch

Easiest Cinnamon-Raisin Rolls

Brew a pot of coffee and share these wonderful rolls with your neighborhood pals.

Makes one dozen

2 c. biscuit baking mix
1/2 c. raisins
1/2 c. sour cream
4 T. milk, divided
2 T. butter, softened
1/2 c. brown sugar, packed
1/4 c. nuts, finely chopped
1/2 t. cinnamon
1 c. powdered sugar

In a bowl, stir together baking mix, raisins, sour cream and 3 tablespoons milk, just until combined. Gently smooth dough into a ball on a floured tea towel. Knead 10 times. Roll dough into a 12-inch by 10-inch rectangle. Spread rectangle with softened butter. Mix brown sugar, nuts and cinnamon; sprinkle over dough. Starting on the long end, roll up dough tightly; pinch edge to seal. Cut roll into 12 slices. Place slices, cut-side down, in greased muffin cups. Bake at 400 degrees for 15 minutes, or until golden. Stir together remaining milk and powdered sugar; drizzle over warm rolls. Makes one dozen.

Cheesy Hashbrown Nuggets

Staci Prickett, Montezuma, GA

Dutch Baby with Spiced Fruit

This is an amazing recipe...everyone loves to watch it bake! It puffs up in the oven, then slightly falls when you take it out. I often make this as a late night treat when I want something a little sweet.

Serves 4 to 6

3 T. butter
1/2 c. all-purpose flour
1 T. sugar
1/4 t. salt
1/8 t. nutmeg
1/2 c. milk, room temperature
2 eggs, room temperature, beaten
1 t. vanilla extract
1/8 t. lemon extract
Garnish: powdered sugar

Add butter to a cast-iron skillet; place in oven at 425 degrees to melt. In a bowl, whisk together flour, sugar, salt and spice. Stir in milk, eggs and extracts; whisk until smooth. Remove hot skillet from oven; swirl butter to evenly coat bottom of skillet. Pour batter into skillet. Bake at 425 degrees for 15 to 18 minutes, until puffy and golden on edges and spots in the center. Remove from oven. Slice and serve, topped with a spoonful of Spiced Fruit and a dusting of powdered sugar.

Spiced Fruit:

2 T. butter
4 apples and/or pears, peeled, cored and sliced 1/4-inch thick
1/4 c. brown sugar, packed
1 t. cornstarch
1 t. apple pie spice
2 T. lemon juice or water

Melt butter in a skillet over medium-high heat. Add apples or pears; stir until coated with butter. Cook for about 5 minutes, until fruit begins to soften. Stir together remaining ingredients; add to skillet. Cook for another 10 minutes, stirring occasionally, or until fruit is tender and sauce has thickened. Remove from heat; let cool slightly.

★ SUPER SKILLETS ★ Watch for old cast-iron skillets at barn sales...they're worth their weight in gold. Often they just need a light scrub, then re-season by brushing lightly with oil and baking at 350 degrees for one hour. Let cool in the oven...all ready to use!

Dutch Baby with Spiced Fruit

Terri Carr, Lewes, DE

Poached Pesto Eggs

I'm always looking for new ideas for my husband's breakfast. I thought pesto and eggs would be a good combination. He loved it!

Serves one to 2

2 eggs
2 to 3 T. basil pesto sauce
2 slices bread, toasted
2 to 4 slices tomato
Garnish: fresh parsley, chopped

Add 2 inches water to a skillet. Bring to a simmer over high heat. One egg at a time, break eggs into a cup and slide into simmering water. Cook eggs for 3 to 5 minutes, to desired doneness. Spread pesto over toast slices; top with tomato slices. With a slotted spoon, top each slice with an egg. Sprinkle with parsley.

Audrey Lett, Newark, DE

Suzanne's Tomato Melt

Start your day with fresh garden flavor...hearty and delicious!

Makes one serving

1/4 c. shredded Cheddar cheese
1 onion bagel or English muffin, split
2 tomato slices
1 T. shredded Parmesan cheese

Sprinkle half the Cheddar cheese over each bagel or English muffin half. Top with a tomato slice. Sprinkle half the Parmesan cheese over each tomato. Broil about 6 inches from heat for 4 to 5 minutes, until cheese is bubbly.

★ TOSS 'EM IN! ★ Add frozen mixed veggies to egg dishes, breakfast casseroles or even fried potatoes for breakfast with a veggie punch!

Poached Pesto Eggs

Leona Krivda, Belle Vernon, PA

Pumpkin Breakfast Cookies

These are great for starting off the day with a cup of hot coffee or tea... yummy for snacking too. This makes a good-size cookie. If you want them smaller, just use a smaller scoop and don't bake as long.

Makes one dozen

1/4 c. coconut oil
1/4 c. honey
1 c. long-cooking oats, uncooked
1 c. quick-cooking oats, uncooked
2/3 c. dried cranberries
2/3 c. pumpkin seeds
1/4 c. ground flax seed
1 t. pumpkin pie spice
1/2 t. salt
1/2 c. canned pumpkin
2 eggs, beaten

Combine coconut oil with honey in a small bowl; microwave just until melted and set aside. In a large bowl, combine all oats, cranberries, pumpkin seeds, flax seed, spice and salt; stir to mix. Add pumpkin, eggs and warm coconut oil mixture; stir until well blended. Drop dough by 1/4-cup scoops onto a parchment paper-lined cookie sheet. Flatten each scoop (cookies will not spread). Bake at 325 degrees for 15 to 20 minutes, until edges are golden. Cool cookies on baking sheet; remove to an airtight container.

★ FLAVOR BOOST ★ Butter-flavored non-stick vegetable spray is especially handy at breakfast time. Use it to spray a skillet for cooking eggs, a waffle iron, pancake griddle or baking pan.

Pumpkin Breakfast Cookies

Vickie, Gooseberry Patch

Cheddar & Bacon Breakfast Sandwiches

Substitute Monterey Jack or Swiss cheese for a variety of flavor!

Makes 4 servings

3 eggs, beaten
1/4 c. milk
2 T. butter
8 thick slices bread
12 slices Cheddar cheese
1/2 T. chopped walnuts
4 slices bacon, crisply cooked and crumbled

In a large bowl, whisk together eggs and milk; set aside. Prepare a griddle or large skillet by melting butter over low heat. Dip only one side of 4 bread slices in egg mixture. Place 4 bread slices, coated side down, on griddle or in skillet. Top each bread slice with 3 cheese slices. Sprinkle cheese with an equal amount of walnuts and bacon. Dip only one side of the remaining 4 bread slices in egg mixture and place over walnuts and bacon, coated side up. Cook 5 minutes per side, or until bread is golden and cheese is melted.

Heather Nagel, Cleveland, OH

Apple-Sausage Pancakes

I first had these at my friend Beth's house for brunch. They were so good! A couple years later at my bridal shower, I was so happy to find this recipe taped to the griddle she bought me as a gift.

Makes one dozen pancakes

1/2 lb. ground pork breakfast sausage
1 egg, beaten
1 c. pancake mix
2/3 c. oil
1/2 t. cinnamon
1/2 c. apple, cored and shredded

Brown sausage in a skillet over medium heat; drain. Meanwhile, in a bowl, mix together egg, pancake mix, oil and cinnamon. Fold in sausage and apple. Drop batter by 1/2 cupfuls onto a hot greased griddle. Cook until golden on both sides. Serve with Apple Syrup.

Apple Syrup:

1 c. apple cider or apple juice
1/2 c. sugar
3 T. butter, sliced
1 T. cornstarch
1 T. lemon juice
1/8 t. pumpkin pie spice

Combine all ingredients in a saucepan over medium-high heat. Stir well and bring to a boil. Reduce heat to low; keep warm until ready to serve.

Cheddar & Bacon Breakfast Sandwiches

Bruce Benton, Tampa, FL

Fried Egg & Cheese Burger

When it's my turn to cook breakfast, this is what I like to make. The kids love having cheeseburgers for breakfast!

Makes 8 servings

1 lb. bacon
2 lbs. ground beef
1/2 t. salt
1/4 t. pepper
1/4 t. garlic powder
8 eggs
Optional: 1 T. butter
8 hamburger buns, split
8 slices cheese
Garnish: lettuce leaves, sliced onion,
    sliced tomato, pickle chips

In a large skillet over medium heat, cook bacon until crisp; drain and set aside. Meanwhile, in a large bowl, sprinkle beef with seasonings; form into 8 patties. In the same skillet over medium heat, cook patties until no longer pink inside. Drain and set aside. Gently crack 4 eggs into the same skillet, adding butter if desired. Cook over medium-low heat until whites are set and yolks are partially cooked; set aside. Cook remaining eggs. To serve, top the bottom of each bun with a beef patty and a cheese slice; place on a broiler pan. Broil until cheese is melted. Top each with one fried egg and 2 slices bacon; add desired garnishes and top halves of buns.

★ HOT TIP ★ Burger buns just taste better toasted...and they won't get soggy! Butter buns lightly and place them on a hot grill for 30 seconds to one minute on each side, until toasty.

Fried Egg & Cheese Burger

Zoe Bennett, Columbia, SC

Sweet & Spicy Bacon

Try this easy-to-fix bacon at your next brunch...guests will love it!

Serves 4 to 5

1/2 c. brown sugar, packed
2 T. chili powder
1 t. ground cumin
1 t. cumin seed
1 t. ground coriander
1/4 t. cayenne pepper
10 thick slices bacon

Line a 15"x10" jelly-roll pan with aluminum foil. Place a wire rack on pan and set aside. Combine all ingredients except bacon. Sprinkle mixture onto a large piece of wax paper. Press bacon slices into mixture, turning to coat well. Arrange in a single layer on wire rack in pan; place pan on center rack of oven. Bake at 400 degrees for 12 minutes; turn bacon over. Bake for 10 more minutes, or until deep brown but not burned. Drain on paper towels; serve warm.

Stephanie Mayer, Portsmouth, VA

Hearty Hashbrowns

Use leftover cooked potatoes from dinner for a speedy start.

Serves 6 to 8

8 slices bacon, crisply cooked,
    crumbled and drippings reserved
10 c. potatoes, peeled, cooked and
    cubed
3 onions, sliced
salt and pepper to taste

In a large skillet, heat reserved drippings over medium heat. Add potatoes and onions to skillet. Cook until potatoes are golden and onions are tender, about 25 minutes. Add salt and pepper to taste; stir in reserved bacon.

★ FREEZE IT ★ If you're cooking up bacon, why not cook up the whole package? Cooked bacon can easily be frozen. Wrap individual portions in paper towels to cushion, then place the towel-wrapped portions into plastic zipping bags. Freeze and store for up to six weeks.

Sweet & Spicy Bacon

Jo Ann, Gooseberry Patch

Sausage Gravy & Biscuits

Enjoy these light and fluffy biscuits topped with hot sausage gravy any time of the day.

Serves 10 to 12

1/2 c. all-purpose flour
2 lbs. ground pork sausage, browned
  and drained
4 c. milk
salt and pepper to taste

In a medium saucepan over medium heat, sprinkle flour over sausage, stirring until flour is dissolved. Gradually stir in milk and cook over medium heat until thick and bubbly. Season with salt and pepper; serve over warm Biscuits.

Biscuits:

4 c. self-rising flour
3 T. baking powder
2 T. sugar
7 T. shortening
2 c. buttermilk

Sift together flour, baking powder and sugar; cut in shortening. Mix in buttermilk with a fork, just until dough is moistened. Shape dough into a ball and knead a few times on a lightly floured surface. Roll out to 3/4-inch thickness and cut with a 3-inch biscuit cutter. Place biscuits on a greased baking sheet. Bake at 450 degrees for about 15 minutes or until golden.

★ EASY SWAP ★ No self-rising flour in the pantry? Try this! To equal one cup self-rising flour, substitute one cup all-purpose flour plus 1-1/2 teaspoons baking powder and 1/2 teaspoon salt.

Sausage Gravy & Biscuits

Lily James, Fort Wayne, IN

Steak & Egg Hash

This is a hearty breakfast my family really loves.

Serves 3 to 6

1 to 2 T. olive oil
1-1/2 lbs. beef sirloin steak, cut
    into 1-inch cubes
1/4 t. salt
1/4 t. pepper
1/4 t. garlic powder
1 lb. potatoes, peeled and diced
1 onion, chopped
3 to 6 eggs
1 c. tomatoes, diced

Heat oil in a skillet over medium heat. Add beef cubes; sprinkle with seasonings. Cook beef cubes until no longer pink. Remove beef to a plate, reserving drippings in skillet. Add potatoes to skillet; cook until golden, stirring occasionally. Add onion; cook until soft and potatoes are cooked through. Return beef to skillet; reduce heat to low. With the back of a spoon, make 3 to 6 shallow wells in potato mixture; gently crack an egg into each well. Sprinkle with tomatoes. Cover and cook until eggs reach desired doneness.

Amy Butcher, Columbus, GA

Fluffy Baked Eggs

Who would have thought to combine pineapple and eggs? After you taste this yummy recipe, you'll see why it is our family favorite!

Makes 12 servings

14 eggs, beaten
3 slices bacon, crisply cooked and
    crumbled
1-1/3 c. low-fat cottage cheese
8-oz. can crushed pineapple in juice,
    drained
1 t. vanilla extract
Garnish: cooked bacon crumbles,
    chopped fresh parsley

Blend together eggs, bacon, cottage cheese, pineapple and vanilla; spoon into a greased 13"x9" baking pan. Bake, uncovered, at 350 degrees for 40 to 45 minutes, until center is set and a toothpick inserted in center comes out clean. Allow baking pan to stand 5 minutes before slicing. Garnish with cooked bacon crumbles and parsley as desired; cut into squares

★ TIME-SAVING SHORTCUT ★ When guests are coming for brunch, a little kitchen prep the night before is really helpful. Whisk up eggs for scrambling, dice meat and potatoes and lay out tableware ahead of time. In the morning, just tie on your prettiest apron and you'll be a relaxed hostess!

Steak & Egg Hash

Kris Coburn, Dansville, NY

Strawberry Cheesecake French Toast

Two favorite foods in one dish... strawberries and cheesecake. Now that's something to wake up to!

Makes 4 servings

1/2 c. cream cheese, softened
2 T. powdered sugar
2 T. strawberry preserves
8 slices country white bread
2 eggs
1/2 c. half-and-half
2 T. sugar
4 T. butter, divided

Combine cream cheese and powdered sugar in a small bowl; mix well. Stir in preserves. Spread cream cheese mixture evenly over 4 slices of bread; top with remaining slices to form sandwiches. Whisk together eggs, half-and-half and sugar in a medium bowl; set aside. Melt 2 tablespoons butter in a large skillet over medium heat. Dip each sandwich into egg mixture, completely covering both sides. Cook 2 sandwiches at a time for one to 2 minutes per side, or until golden. Melt remaining butter and cook remaining sandwiches as instructed.

Gladys Kielar, Whitehouse, OH

Birthday Baked French Swirl Toast

We've enjoyed this baked French toast for birthday breakfasts. It's a great choice for any special day and when guests come for an overnight visit.

Makes 8 servings

16-oz. loaf cinnamon swirl bread, cubed
3/4 c. sweetened dried cranberries
6 eggs, beaten
3 c. half-and-half or milk
2 t. vanilla extract
Garnish: cinnamon-sugar or powdered sugar, whipped butter, maple syrup

Combine bread cubes and cranberries in a greased shallow 3-quart casserole dish. In a bowl, whisk together eggs, half-and-half or milk and vanilla; pour over bread mixture. Cover and refrigerate for one hour to overnight. Uncover; bake at 350 degrees for 45 minutes, or until golden and set in the center. Sprinkle with cinnamon-sugar or powdered sugar. Serve topped with whipped butter and maple syrup.

Strawberry Cheesecake French Toast

Paula Johnson, Center City, M

Cinnamon-Pumpkin Pancakes

Everyone loves this cinnamon and pumpkin combination. Yum!

Makes 2 dozen, serves 6

1 c. whole-wheat flour
1 T. sugar
2 t. baking powder
1/4 t. salt
1/2 t. cinnamon
1 c. skim milk
1/2 c. canned pumpkin
2 eggs, separated and divided
1-1/2 T. oil

In a large mixing bowl, combine flour, sugar, baking powder, salt and cinnamon. In a separate bowl, blend together milk, pumpkin, beaten egg yolks and oil. Add pumpkin mixture to flour mixture all at once, stirring until just blended. Beat egg whites with an electric mixer on high speed until stiff peaks form, then gently fold into pancake batter. For each pancake, spoon 2 to 3 tablespoons batter onto a griddle sprayed with non-stick vegetable spray. Cook until bubbles begin to form around edges; turn and cook until second side is golden.

Jennifer Bontrager, Oklahoma City, OK

Yummy Blueberry Waffles

When I was a little girl, my grandpa owned a blueberry farm. The berries were so delicious that we always took home several gallons when our summer visit was over. This waffle recipe cooks up nice and fluffy...and the farm-fresh blueberries only make them better!

Makes 4 waffles

2 eggs
2 c. all-purpose flour
1-3/4 c. milk
1/2 c. oil
1 T. sugar
4 t. baking powder
1/4 t. salt
1/2 t. vanilla extract
1 to 1-1/2 c. blueberries

In a large bowl, beat eggs with an electric mixer on medium speed until fluffy. Add remaining ingredients except berries; beat just until smooth. Spray a waffle iron with non-stick vegetable spray. Pour batter by 1/2 cupfuls onto the preheated waffle iron. Scatter desired amount of berries over batter. Bake according to manufacturer's directions, until golden.

Cinnamon-Pumpkin Pancakes

Lizzy Burnley, Ankeny, IA

Lizzy's Make-Ahead Egg Casserole

This recipe is a favorite for breakfast, lunch or dinner. And preparing it ahead makes it that much easier! It is perfect for serving after the Easter egg hunt or for a Mother's Day brunch.

Serves 12

1 doz. eggs, beaten
1 c. cooked ham, diced
3 c. whole milk
12 frozen waffles, divided
2 c. shredded Cheddar cheese, divided

In a large bowl, beat eggs. Stir in ham and milk. Grease a 13"x9" baking pan. Place one layer of waffles in the bottom of the pan. Pour half of the mixture on the waffles. Sprinkle with half of the cheese. Continue layering waffles, egg mixture and cheese. Cover and refrigerate overnight. Uncover and bake at 350 degrees for about one hour or until eggs are set.

Melissa Cassulis, Bridgewater, NY

Haystack Eggs

This is one of my dad's favorite breakfast treats. Mom has been making it for him for almost as long as I can remember!

Makes 4 servings

1-3/4 oz. can shoestring potatoes
4 eggs
1 c. shredded Cheddar cheese
6 slices bacon, crisply cooked and
   crumbled

Spread potatoes evenly over bottom of a greased 9" pie plate. Make 4 indentations in potatoes almost to bottom of pie plate. Carefully break one egg into each indentation. Bake at 350 degrees for 8 to 10 minutes, until eggs are almost set. Sprinkle with cheese and bacon. Return to oven; bake 2 to 4 more minutes, until eggs are set and cheese melts. Cut into 4 wedges; serve immediately.

★ BREAKFAST FOR DINNER ★ Breakfast foods are so warm and comforting...try 'em for dinner as a special treat! Scrambled eggs and toast or pancakes and bacon are easy to stir up in minutes. Or assemble a family-favorite breakfast casserole in the morning and pop it in the oven at dinnertime.

Lizzy's Make-Ahead Egg Casserole

Mary Ann Lewis, Olive Branch, MS

Best-Ever Breakfast Bars

These chewy, healthy bars are perfect to grab in the morning for a perfect take-along breakfast.

Makes one dozen

1 c. favorite granola
1 c. quick-cooking oats, uncooked
1/2 c. all-purpose flour
1/4 c. brown sugar, packed
1/8 t. cinnamon
1/2 c. unsalted mixed nuts, coarsely chopped
1/2 c. dried fruit, chopped into small pieces
2 T. ground flaxseed meal
1/4 c. canola oil
1/3 c. honey
1/2 t. vanilla extract
1 egg, beaten

Combine granola and the next 7 ingredients in a large bowl. Whisk together oil, honey and vanilla; stir into granola mixture. Add egg; stir to blend. Press mixture into a parchment paper-lined 9"x7" sheet pan. Bake at 325 degrees for 30 to 35 minutes, until lightly golden around the edges. Remove from oven and cool 30 minutes to one hour. Slice into bars.

Carol Hickman, Kingsport, TN

Fried Green Tomato Biscuits

These southern classics are great for a summertime breakfast or brunch! Try one with a tall glass of sweet tea.

Serves 4 to 8

16-oz. tube refrigerated buttermilk biscuits
1/2 lb. bacon
1 c. buttermilk
1-1/2 c. self-rising cornmeal
salt and pepper to taste
2 green tomatoes, thickly sliced
Garnish: mayonnaise

Bake biscuits according to package directions; set aside. In a large skillet, cook bacon until crisp; remove to paper towels to drain, reserving drippings in skillet. Pour buttermilk into a shallow bowl. On a small plate, combine cornmeal, salt and pepper. Dip tomato slices into buttermilk and then cornmeal mixture, until thickly coated on both sides. Fry tomatoes in reserved drippings over medium-high heat for 4 minutes per side, or until golden. Drain on paper towels. Split biscuits; spread one biscuit half with mayonnaise. Top with a tomato slice, bacon and top half of biscuit.

Best-Ever Breakfast Bars

Linda Picard, Newport, OR

Savory Oatmeal Bowls with Egg, Bacon & Kale

This one-bowl breakfast will give you a jump-start for a busy day at school or work.

Serves 2

2 slices bacon, diced
1 bunch kale, thinly sliced
1/2 c. tomato, diced
1 t. red wine vinegar
1/8 t. salt
1 c. cooked steel-cut oats
1/3 c. avocado, peeled, pitted and diced
1 t. olive oil
2 eggs
1/8 t. pepper
Optional: 1/2 t. hot pepper sauce

In a large skillet over medium heat, cook bacon until almost crisp, stirring occasionally. Add kale; cook for 2 to 4 minutes, until wilted. Stir in tomato, vinegar and salt. Divide oats evenly between 2 bowls. Top with kale mixture and avocado; set aside. Wipe skillet clean with a paper towel; return to medium heat. Add oil and swirl to coat. Crack eggs into skillet, one at a time; cook for 2 minutes. Cover and cook for one minute, or until whites are set. Top each bowl with one egg. Sprinkle with pepper and hot sauce, if using.

Becky Woods, Ballwin, MO

Smoked Gouda Grits

These smoky and creamy grits are the perfect addition to scrambled eggs and breakfast sausage...yum!

Serves 6 to 8

6 c. chicken broth
2 c. milk
1 t. salt
1/2 t. white pepper
2 c. quick-cooking grits, uncooked
1-2/3 c. shredded smoked Gouda cheese
3 T. butter, softened

Bring broth, milk, salt and pepper to a boil in a large saucepan over medium heat. Gradually whisk in grits. Reduce heat; cover and simmer, stirring occasionally, about 5 minutes or until thickened. Add cheese and butter; stir until melted.

★ SPRINKLE IT! ★ For a nutty taste and extra fiber, sprinkle wheat germ or flax seed onto servings of oatmeal. Tastes great too.

Savory Oatmeal Bowls with Egg, Bacon & Kale

Eleanor Dionne, Beverly, MA

Blueberry Cornmeal Pancakes

Since we like cornmeal muffins as well as anything with blueberries, it's no surprise that these pancakes became a family favorite.

Makes about 24 pancakes

1 c. all-purpose flour
1 c. cornmeal
2 T. baking powder
1 T. sugar
1-1/2 c. orange juice
3 T. canola oil
1 egg, beaten
1 c. blueberries, thawed if frozen
Garnish: fresh blueberries, light
   maple syrup

In a bowl, mix together flour, cornmeal, baking powder and sugar. Add juice, oil and egg; stir well. Gently fold in blueberries. Heat a lightly greased griddle over medium-high heat. Pour batter onto griddle, making small pancakes. Cook pancakes until bubbles appear around the edges; flip and cook on other side. Garnish as desired.

Amy Tucker, British Columbia, Canada

Peanut Butter Muffins

These will become your family's favorite muffins. They are so moist and full of peanut-buttery flavor!

Makes 1-1/2 dozen

1 c. whole-wheat flour
1 c. long-cooking oats, uncooked
1-1/2 t. baking soda
1/4 c. creamy peanut butter
1/3 c. applesauce
1-1/2 c. skim milk
1/4 c. honey
2 T. finely chopped peanuts

Whisk together flour, oats and baking soda. Add peanut butter and applesauce; beat with an electric mixer on low speed until smooth. Stir in milk and honey. Spoon batter into paper-lined or greased muffin cups, filling 2/3 full. Sprinkle with chopped peanuts. Bake at 350 degrees for 12 to 15 minutes, until a toothpick tests clean. Cool in pan 5 minutes; transfer to a wire rack to finish cooling.

Blueberry Cornmeal Pancakes

Beth Kramer, Port St. Lucie, FL

Orange Coffee Rolls

Perfect for Christmas morning, these rolls are our family favorite.

Makes 2 dozen

1 env. active dry yeast
1/4 c. warm water, 110 to 115 degrees
1 c. sugar, divided
2 eggs, beaten
1/2 c. sour cream
1/4 c. plus 2 T. butter, melted
1 t. salt
2-3/4 to 3 c. all-purpose flour
2 T. butter, melted and divided
1 c. flaked coconut, toasted and
  divided
2 T. orange zest

Combine the yeast and the warm water in a large bowl; let stand 5 minutes. Add 1/4 cup sugar and next 4 ingredients; beat at medium speed with an electric mixer until blended. Gradually stir in enough flour to make a soft dough. Turn dough out onto a well-floured surface; knead until smooth and elastic (about 5 minutes). Place in a well-greased bowl, turning to grease top. Cover and let rise in a warm place (85 degrees), free from drafts, 1-1/2 hours or until double in bulk. Punch dough down and divide in half. Roll one portion of dough into a 12-inch circle; brush with one tablespoon melted butter. Combine remaining sugar, 3/4 cup coconut and orange zest; sprinkle half of coconut mixture over dough. Cut into 12 wedges; roll up each wedge, beginning at wide end. Place in a greased 13"x9" baking pan, point-side down. Repeat with remaining dough, butter and coconut mixture. Cover and let rise in a warm place, free from drafts, 45 minutes or until double in bulk. Bake at 350 degrees for 25 to 30 minutes or until golden. (Cover with aluminum foil after 15 minutes to prevent excessive browning, if necessary.) Spoon warm Glaze over warm rolls; sprinkle with remaining coconut.

Glaze:

3/4 c. sugar
1/2 c. sour cream
1/4 c. butter
2 t. orange juice

Combine all ingredients in a small saucepan; bring to a boil. Boil 3 minutes, stirring occasionally. Let cool slightly. Makes 1-1/3 cups.

Orange Coffee Rolls

Emily Martin, Ontario, Canada

Sleep-Over Breakfast Strata

Every year at Christmas, we're sure to have some of my relatives staying for the holidays. This recipe fills up our hungry crowd, and everyone loves it.

Serves 8 to 10

4 c. day-old white bread, cubed
8 eggs
1-1/2 c. milk
1/2 t. salt
1/2 t. pepper
8-oz. pkg. shredded Cheddar cheese
8-oz. pkg. sliced mushrooms
3/4 lb. bacon, crisply cooked and
   crumbled

Place bread in a 6-quart slow cooker sprayed with a non-stick vegetable spray; set aside. Beat eggs in a large bowl. Whisk in milk, salt and pepper; stir in cheese and mushrooms. Pour egg mixture evenly over bread; set aside. Cook bacon in a skillet over medium heat until crisp; drain, crumble and sprinkle over top. Cover and cook on low setting for 6 to 8 hours, until eggs have set and top is lightly golden. Uncover and let stand for several minutes before serving.

Judy Zechman, Butler, PA

Baked Shrimp & Grits

This recipe is a grits-lover's dream come true! It's so savory and tasty, but still really easy to prepare.

Serves 4 to 6

5 c. water
1-1/4 c. quick-cooking grits,
   uncooked
2 c. shredded Cheddar cheese
1/2 c. butter
2 eggs, beaten
1 c. milk
garlic powder and salt to taste
1 lb. uncooked medium shrimp,
   peeled and cleaned
2 T. olive oil
1/2 c. white wine or chicken broth
2 t. garlic, minced
1-1/2 t. fresh parsley, chopped
1/4 t. salt
1/2 t. pepper
4 T. lemon juice

Bring water to a boil in a saucepan over medium-high heat. Cook grits in boiling water for 5 minutes. Add cheese, butter, eggs, milk, garlic powder and salt to grits; mix well. Spoon into a greased 4-quart casserole dish. Bake, uncovered, at 350 degrees for 45 minutes, or until lightly golden. Meanwhile, in a skillet over medium heat, sauté shrimp in olive oil until cooked through. Add remaining ingredients; heat through. Top grits with shrimp before serving.

Sleep-Over Breakfast Strata

Sheila Plock, Boalsburg, PA

Creamy Cinnamon Rolls

These delectable bites make a great breakfast treat anytime. You can even make the dough ahead of time. Just place rolls in the pan, cover with greased plastic wrap, refrigerate overnight and let them rise the following morning until double in bulk, approximately two hours.

Makes 20 rolls

16-oz. pkg. frozen white bread dough,
  thawed
2 T. butter, melted
2/3 c. brown sugar, packed
1/2 c. chopped nuts
1 t. cinnamon
1/2 c. whipping cream
2/3 c. powdered sugar
1 T. milk

Roll dough into an 18"x6" rectangle on a lightly floured surface. Brush with melted butter. Combine brown sugar, nuts and cinnamon. Sprinkle evenly over dough. Roll up jelly-roll style, starting with a long side. Cut into 20 slices; arrange cut-side down in a greased 13"x9" baking pan. Cover and let rise until almost double in bulk, about 1-1/2 hours. Uncover and pour cream over rolls. Bake at 350 degrees for 25 to 30 minutes. Mix together powdered sugar and milk; drizzle over warm rolls.

Laura Carter, Vinita, OK

Overnight Caramel Pecan Rolls

I got this recipe from my grandmother and mother...it's a family favorite that we all enjoy.

Serves 10 to 12

2 3.4-oz. pkgs. instant
  butterscotch pudding mix
1 c. brown sugar, packed
1 c. chopped pecans
1/2 c. chilled butter
36 frozen rolls, divided

Combine dry pudding mixes, brown sugar and pecans in a bowl. Cut in butter; set aside. Arrange half the frozen rolls in a lightly greased Bundt® pan. Sprinkle half the pudding mixture over top. Repeat layering with remaining rolls and pudding mixture. Cover loosely; refrigerate overnight. Bake at 350 degrees for one hour. Invert onto a serving plate.

Creamy Cinnamon Rolls

Robin Long, Newberry, SC

Cream Cheese Danish

Did you get out of bed on the wrong side today? You'll feel so much better after you've tasted this!

Serves 15 to 20

2 8-oz. pkgs. cream cheese, softened
3/4 c. sugar
1 egg yolk, beaten
2 t. lemon juice
1 t. vanilla extract
2 8-oz. tubes refrigerated crescent
    rolls
2 c. powdered sugar
4 to 5 T. milk

Blend together cream cheese and sugar in a large bowl; add egg yolk, lemon juice and vanilla. Set aside. Layer one tube of crescent rolls in bottom of a greased 13"x9" baking pan; press seams together. Spread cream cheese mixture over top; layer remaining tube of rolls on top of cream cheese. Bake at 350 degrees for 15 to 20 minutes, until golden. Let cool. Mix together powdered sugar and milk to a thin consistency; drizzle over top. Cut into slices to serve.

Carol Doiron, North Berwick, ME

Swirled Coffee Cake

A boxed mix makes this delicious coffee cake a breeze to prepare!

Serves 12 to 15

18-1/4 oz. pkg. yellow cake mix
5-1/4 oz. pkg. instant pistachio
    pudding mix
4 eggs, beaten
1 t. vanilla extract
1 c. water
1/2 c. oil
1/2 c. sugar
2 t. cinnamon
1/2 c. chopped walnuts

Combine dry cake mix and dry pudding mix in a large bowl; blend in eggs, vanilla, water and oil. Pour half the batter into a greased Bundt® pan; set aside. Mix together sugar, cinnamon and walnuts in a small bowl; sprinkle half over batter in pan. Swirl in with a knife; add remaining batter. Swirl in remaining sugar mixture. Bake at 350 degrees for 50 minutes, or until cake tests done with a toothpick. Cool in pan and remove to a serving platter.

Cream Cheese Danish

Tomato-Tortellini Soup, Page 124

CHAPTER THREE

All-Star Soups, Muffins & Breads

Cheddar-Chive Muffins, Page 118

Chicken & Dumplin' Soup, Page 108

Kay Little, Diana, TX

Blue-Ribbon 8-Hour Chili

When my church announced they were having a chili cook-off, I knew I had to enter...but I needed to name this recipe. I came up with the name because it takes 8 hours to cook to perfection. Going into the contest, it was just 8-Hour Chili, but coming out of the contest, it became Blue-Ribbon 8-hour Chili. To my delight, I won first place!

Serves 10 to 12

3 lbs. lean ground beef
1 T. salt
1 T. pepper
15-oz. can ranch-style beans
14-1/2 oz. can diced tomatoes
10-oz. can diced tomatoes with
  green chiles
4 8-oz. cans tomato sauce

8 green onions, chopped
1/2 c. onion, minced
4 pickled jalapeños, seeded and
  minced
1/4 c. pickled jalapeño juice
1/4 c. chili seasoning mix
1 T. ground cumin
2 c. water
Garnish: shredded Cheddar cheese,
  diced red onion, oyster crackers

Brown beef in a large skillet over medium heat; season with salt and pepper. Drain and spoon beef mixture into a slow cooker. Add undrained beans, undrained tomatoes and remaining ingredients except garnish to slow cooker in order listed; stir. Cover and cook on high setting, stirring occasionally, for 7 to 8 hours. Garnish servings with cheese, onion and crackers.

★ TOO HOT! ★ If you've added a bit too much hot chili seasoning to the chili, it's easy to cool it off. Simply stir a tablespoon each of lemon or lime juice and sugar into the chili.

Blue-Ribbon 8-Hour Chili

Jo Ann, Gooseberry Patch

Sweet Potato Cornbread

This rich cornbread is sure to become your family favorite. Baking in a skillet makes the edges so wonderfully golden. Serve it with honey butter or raspberry jam.

Makes 6 servings

2 c. self-rising cornmeal mix
1/4 c. sugar
1 t. cinnamon
1-1/2 c. milk
1 c. cooked sweet potato, mashed
1/4 c. butter, melted
1 egg, beaten

Whisk together all ingredients just until dry ingredients are moistened. Spoon the batter into a greased 8" cast-iron skillet or pan. Bake at 425 degrees for 30 minutes, or until a toothpick inserted in center comes out clean.

Lois Hobart, Stone Creek, OH

Lemon-Rosemary Zucchini Bread

This zucchini bread is the best! It smells wonderful while it bakes and tastes so good. Mini loaves or muffins make a nice gift.

Makes 2 loaves or 2 dozen muffins

3 c. all-purpose flour
1/2 t. baking powder
2 t. baking soda
2 T. fresh rosemary, minced
2 eggs
1-1/4 c. sugar
1/2 c. butter, melted and slightly cooled
1/4 c. olive oil
1 T. lemon zest
3 c. zucchini, grate

In a bowl, whisk together flour, baking powder, baking soda and rosemary; set aside. In a separate large bowl, beat eggs until frothy; beat in sugar, melted butter and olive oil. Stir in lemon zest and zucchini. Add flour mixture to egg mixture; stir until blended. Divide batter into two 9"x4" loaf pans sprayed with non-stick vegetable spray. Bake at 350 degrees for 45 to 50 minutes. May also spoon batter into 24 paper-lined muffin cups, filling 2/3 full; bake at 350 degrees for 20 minutes.

Sweet Potato Cornbread

Lynda Robson, Boston, MA

New England Fish Chowder

Garnish chowder with oyster crackers and chopped fresh parsley. Add a little chopped bacon for a more smoky flavor.

Makes 6 servings

1 T. oil
1/2 c. onion, chopped
2-1/2 c. potatoes, peeled and diced
1-1/2 c. boiling water
salt and pepper to taste
1 lb. frozen cod or haddock
    fillets, thawed and cut into
    large chunks
2 c. milk
1 T. butter
Garnish: fresh parsley

Heat oil in a large saucepan over medium heat. Add onion; cook until tender. Add potatoes, water, salt and pepper. Reduce heat; cover and simmer for 15 to 20 minutes, until potatoes are tender. Add fish; simmer until fish flakes easily with a fork, about 5 minutes. Add milk and butter just before serving; heat through. Garnish with fresh parsley.

Jan Durston, Norco, CA

Jan's Prize-Winning Chili

This recipe won a chili cook-off at my church. Every Halloween I make it in a slow cooker and then set it to warm... that way everyone can eat either before or after trick-or-treating.

Serves 10 to 12

1-1/2 lbs. ground beef
1 onion, chopped
1 clove garlic, minced
29-oz. can tomato sauce
28-oz. can diced tomatoes
16-oz. can pinto beans, drained and
    rinsed
16-oz. can red kidney beans,
    drained and rinsed
7-oz. can diced green chiles
2 cubes beef bouillon
2 1-1/4 oz. pkgs. chili seasoning mix
Garnish: shredded Cheddar cheese,
    sour cream, minced onion

Brown beef, onion and garlic in a Dutch oven over medium heat; drain. Mix together remaining ingredients except garnish; add to ground beef mixture. Cover and cook over low heat for at least one hour, stirring occasionally. Top servings with cheese, sour cream and minced onion.

New England Fish Chowder

Kim Bugaj, Manchester, CT

Grandma's Best Cinnamon-Sugar Bread

This is an amazing cinnamon bread! The recipe was handed down from my grandma to my mom, and then Mom handed it down to me. It tastes so good warm.

Makes one loaf

1 T. butter, softened
1-1/3 c. sugar, divided
4 t. cinnamon, divided
2 c. all-purpose flour
1 T. baking powder
3/4 t. salt
1 egg, beaten
1 c. milk
1/3 c. canola oil
1 t. vanilla extract

Coat a 9"x5" loaf pan with butter; set aside. In a small bowl, stir together 1/3 cup sugar and 3 teaspoons cinnamon; set aside. In a large bowl, sift together flour, baking powder, salt and remaining cinnamon and remaining sugar. In another bowl, whisk together egg, milk, oil and vanilla. Add egg mixture to flour mixture; stir just until combined. Pour half of batter into loaf pan; sprinkle with half of cinnamon-sugar. Add remaining batter; use a knife to swirl batter. Top with remaining cinnamon-sugar. Bake at 350 degrees for 45 minutes, or until a toothpick inserted in the center comes out clean. Cool in pan on a wire rack for 10 minutes. Remove loaf from pan onto a plate or small platter. Carefully press all the sides of the loaf into any cinnamon-sugar that comes off onto the plate. Slice and serve.

★ SIMPLE SWAP ★ In most quick breads, brownies, cakes and scones you can substitute measure for measure the fat with puréed fruit, fruit juice, mashed pumpkin or squash, buttermilk, applesauce, prune butter or non-fat yogurt.

Grandma's Best Cinnamon-Sugar Bread

Shirley White, Gatesville, TX

Erma Lee's Chicken Soup

My family requests this soup at the first sign of cold weather.

Serves 4 to 6

3 14-1/2 oz. cans chicken broth
2/3 c. onion, diced
2/3 c. carrot, peeled and diced
2/3 c. celery, diced
2 10-3/4-oz. cans cream of
    mushroom soup
4 boneless, skinless chicken
    breasts, cooked and chopped
8-oz. pkg. pasteurized process
    cheese spread, cubed
1 c. shredded Cheddar cheese
1 c. cooked rice

Bring broth to a boil in a stockpot over medium heat. Add vegetables; cook until tender, about 10 minutes. Stir in remaining ingredients; simmer over low heat until cheeses melt and soup is heated through, about 15 minutes.

Kathy Grashoff, Fort Wayne, IN

Ham & Bean Soup

Our family really enjoys this soup. It's always a welcome lunch after a chilly day in the stands watching football!

Makes 4 servings

1 c. dried navy beans , rinsed and
    sorted
8 c. water, divided
2 stalks celery, sliced
2 carrots, peeled and sliced
1 onion, chopped
3/4 c. cooked ham, cubed
1 t. chicken bouillon granules
1 t. dried thyme
2 bay leaves
1/4 t. pepper

In a large saucepan, combine beans and 4 cups water. Bring to a boil; reduce heat to low. Simmer, uncovered, for 2 minutes. Remove from heat. Cover and let stand for one hour. Drain and rinse beans; return to pan. Add remaining water and remaining ingredients. Bring to a boil; reduce heat to low. Cover and simmer for 1-1/4 hours, or until beans are tender. Discard bay leaves. Using a fork, slightly mash some beans against the side of the saucepan to thicken soup.

Erma Lee's Chicken Soup

Maddie Schaum, Mount Airy, MD

Pasta e Fagioli

The name of this mostly meatless Italian dish means pasta and beans. You'll find many variations that use pancetta or prosciutto...we added bacon to our version.

Makes 6 servings

15-oz. can cannellini beans
2 T. olive oil
3 slices bacon, coarsely chopped
2 stalks celery, chopped
2 carrots, peeled and chopped
1 onion, chopped
2 cloves garlic, minced
3 14-1/2 oz. cans chicken broth
15-oz. can kidney beans,
   drained and rinsed
1 c. small shell pasta, uncooked
salt and pepper to taste
Garnish: 6 T. grated Parmesan
   cheese

Mash undrained cannellini beans with a fork in a bowl and set aside. Heat oil in a large saucepan over medium heat; add bacon and next 4 ingredients. Cook for 7 to 10 minutes, stirring occasionally, until bacon is crisp and vegetables are softened. Add broth, cannellini beans and kidney beans; bring to a boil over high heat. Stir pasta into soup. Reduce heat to medium. Cook, uncovered, for 6 to 8 minutes, stirring frequently, until pasta is tender. Add salt and pepper; top each serving with a tablespoon of cheese.

★ PASTA FUN ★ Tiny pasta shapes like ditalini, orzo, acini di pepe and stelline or stars are all quick-cooking and ideal for making soup. Choose your favorite...you can even substitute alphabets just for fun.

Pasta e Fagioli

Kay Marone, Des Moines, IA

Iowa's Best Corn Chowder

Iowa is corn country, and this soup is a local favorite.

Makes 8 servings

1/2 c. onion, diced
1 clove garlic, minced
1/2 t. ground cumin
1 t. olive oil
4 c. vegetable broth
4 c. corn
2 new potatoes, diced
1/2 t. kosher salt
1/8 t. pepper
3/4 c. milk
1 t. fresh cilantro, chopped

Sauté onion, garlic and cumin in oil in a stockpot over medium heat for 5 minutes, or until onion is tender. Add broth and next 4 ingredients; bring to a boil. Reduce to a simmer and cook for 20 minutes, or until potatoes are tender. Add milk and cilantro; cook and stir to heat through.

★ HANDY TIP ★ Soups and chowders are extra hearty served in bread bowls. Cut the tops off round crusty loaves and scoop out the soft bread inside. Brush with olive oil. Bake at 350 degrees for a few minutes until toasty, then ladle in soup.

Patti Bogetti, Magnolia, DE

Blue-Ribbon Crab & Asparagus Chowder

The recipe has become a tradition at my friend's Barn Bash every fall. Everyone always asks that I bring it every year. Recently, I won the blue ribbon at the state fair in the Chili vs. Chowder Cook-off, yee-haw!

Makes 10 servings

1/2 c. butter
1 sweet onion, chopped
2 carrots, peeled and chopped
3 stalks celery, chopped
1 t. salt
1/2 t. pepper
1/4 c. all-purpose flour
4 c. water
1/2 t. nutmeg
1 t. seafood seasoning
1 T. chicken bouillon granules
3 redskin potatoes, peeled and cubed
4 c. whole milk
2 t. fresh parsley, chopped
3 c. asparagus, trimmed and chopped
1 lb. crabmeat
Optional: additional milk

Melt butter in a large stockpot over medium heat; add onion, carrots, celery, salt and pepper. Continue to cook until vegetables are softened, about 10 minutes. Stir in flour to coat vegetables. Slowly whisk in water; stir in nutmeg, seasoning, bouillon and potatoes. Bring to a boil; reduce heat and simmer, covered, 10 minutes or until potatoes are tender. Add milk, parsley and asparagus. Simmer 10 minutes longer. Gently fold in crabmeat. Heat through. If chowder is too thick, thin with more milk, if desired.

Iowa's Best Corn Chowder

Amanda Kisting, Dubuque, IA

Garlic-Cheddar Beer Biscuits

My family loves the arrival of fall, when these cake-like biscuits reappear on our table. They're perfect with any cold-weather dish... the aroma of the garlic warms the whole house as they bake.

Makes one dozen

1/4 c. butter, sliced
6 cloves garlic, minced
2-1/2 c. self-rising flour
2 T. sugar
12-oz. bottle regular or non-alcoholic beer, room temperature
3/4 c. shredded sharp Cheddar cheese
1/4 t. Italian seasoning

Combine butter and garlic in a microwave-safe dish. Microwave until butter is melted, 30 seconds to one minute. In a large bowl, combine remaining ingredients and garlic mixture. Stir until moistened. Spray a 12-cup muffin tin with non-stick vegetable spray. Divide batter evenly among muffin cups. Bake at 400 degrees for 15 minutes, or until tops just begin to turn golden. Immediately turn biscuits out onto a plate and serve.

Carol Field Dahlstrom, Ankeny, IA

Bacon-Corn Muffins

Little bits of crisp bacon make these muffins a favorite at breakfast or alongside a bowl of soup.

Makes 2 dozen

2-3/4 c. all-purpose flour
3/4 c. sugar
2/3 c. yellow cornmeal
1 t. salt
1 t. baking powder
1/2 t. baking soda
1 c. crisply cooked bacon, cut or broken into 1/4-inch pieces
1-1/2 c. buttermilk
4 eggs, beaten
3/4 c. oil
2/3 c. shredded Cheddar cheese
1/4 c. red or orange sweet peppers, chopped

In a large bowl, combine flour, sugar, cornmeal, salt, baking powder, baking soda and bacon. Make a well in the dry ingredients. Set aside. In a small bowl, mix buttermilk, eggs and oil. Slowly pour egg mixture into flour mixture, stirring until just moistened. Fold in cheese and peppers. Spoon batter into 24 paper-lined or greased muffin cups, filling 3/4 full. Bake at 375 degrees for 20 to 25 minutes, until golden and firm in the center.

Garlic-Cheddar Beer Biscuits

Brenda Hancock, Hartford, KY

Chicken & Dumplin' Soup

Refrigerated biscuits make this ultimate comfort food ever-so easy!

Serves 6 to 8

10-3/4 oz. can cream of chicken soup
4 c. chicken broth
4 boneless, skinless chicken breasts, cooked and shredded
2 15-oz. cans mixed vegetables
12-oz. tube refrigerated biscuits, quartered
Optional: pepper to taste

Combine soup and broth in a 6-quart stockpot; bring to a boil over medium-high heat, whisking until smooth. Stir in chicken and vegetables; bring to a boil. Drop biscuit quarters into soup; cover and simmer for 15 minutes. Let soup stand for 10 minutes before serving. Sprinkle each serving with pepper, if desired.

Cynthia Johnson, Verona, WI

Beefy Vegetable Soup

This slow-cooker soup is so easy to put together. It's delicious and makes your home smell wonderful, especially on chilly fall nights!

Makes 8 servings

1 lb. ground beef
1 onion, chopped
1 clove garlic, minced
16-oz. can kidney beans
16-oz. can cannellini beans
10-oz. pkg. frozen corn & pea blend
14-1/2 oz. can diced tomatoes
2 8-oz. cans tomato sauce
1 c. carrots, peeled and shredded
1 t. chili powder
1/2 t. dried basil
1/2 t. salt
1/4 t. pepper

In a skillet, cook beef, onion and garlic over medium heat until beef is no longer pink; drain. Transfer to a 5-quart slow cooker. Add remaining ingredients; mix well. Cover and cook on low setting for 8 hours, or until thick and bubbly.

Chicken & Dumplin' Soup

Francie Stutzman, Dalton, OH

Italian Bread

We love this bread with homemade vegetable soup or spaghetti...it disappears very quickly!

Makes 3 large loaves

2-1/2 c. water
2 envs. active dry yeast
2 t. salt
1/4 c. sugar
1/4 c. olive oil
7 c. all-purpose flour
1/4 c. cornmeal
1 egg white
1 T. cold water

Heat 2-1/2 cups water until very warm, about 110 to 115 degrees. Dissolve yeast in very warm water in a large bowl. Add salt, sugar and oil; stir well. Stir in flour; mix well. Shape dough into a ball and place in a well-greased bowl, turning to coat top. Cover and let rise one hour, or until double in bulk; punch dough down. Divide dough into 3 equal parts and shape into loaves. Place loaves crosswise on a greased baking sheet that has been sprinkled with cornmeal. Cover and let rise 30 minutes. Cut 4 diagonal slices in the top of each loaf. Bake at 400 degrees for 25 to 30 minutes, until golden. Combine egg white and cold water in a small bowl; whisk well and brush over loaves. Bake 5 more minutes.

Becky Butler, Keller, TX

Best-Ever Southern Cornbread

My whole adult life, I have been searching for the "best-ever" recipe for baked goods that I prepare often. This is the cornbread recipe I've made for 20 years! True Southern cornbread is not sweet, but if you like it sweet, 2 to 3 tablespoons of sugar can be added.

Makes 8 servings

1 c. yellow cornmeal
1/2 c. all-purpose flour
1 t. baking powder
1/2 t. baking soda
1 t. salt
1-1/2 c. buttermilk
2 eggs, beaten
1/4 c. butter, bacon drippings or oil
Garnish: softened butter

Place a 10" cast-iron skillet in 425-degree oven to preheat. In a large bowl, whisk together cornmeal, flour, baking powder, baking soda and salt; set aside. In a small bowl, whisk together buttermilk and eggs. Add buttermilk mixture to cornmeal mixture and stir until just combined; some small lumps are all right. Carefully remove hot skillet from oven; brush with butter, drippings or oil. Pour batter into hot skillet and spread evenly. Bake at 425 degrees for 15 to 18 minutes, until a toothpick inserted into the center comes out clean. Turn cornbread out onto a dinner plate and cut into wedges, or cut into wedges and serve out of the hot skillet. Serve with softened butter.

Italian Bread

Belinda Gibson, Amarillo, TX

Cheesy Vegetable Soup

Oh my goodness...this is the best soup I've ever tasted! And it's so easy to make too.

Serves 10 to 12

4 10-1/2 oz. cans chicken broth
2-1/2 c. potatoes, peeled
    and cubed
1 c. celery, chopped
1 c. onion, chopped
2-1/2 c. broccoli, chopped
2-1/2 c. caulifl ower, chopped
2 10-3/4 oz. cans cream of
    chicken soup
16-oz. pkg. pasteurized process
    cheese spread, cubed
16-oz. pkg. pasteurized process
    Mexican cheese spread, cubed
1 lb. cooked ham, cubed

Combine broth, potatoes, celery and onion in a large soup pot over medium heat. Simmer until vegetables are tender, about 20 minutes. Add broccoli and cauliflower; simmer an additional 10 minutes. Stir in soup, cheeses and ham; simmer until cheeses melt and soup is heated through.

Christian Brown, Killeen, TX

Chicken Broth From Scratch

Everyone needs a good recipe for homemade chicken broth! Use the broth right away in a recipe or freeze for later use.

Makes 8 cups

3 to 4-lb. roasting chicken
2 carrots, peeled and thickly sliced
2 stalks celery, thickly sliced
1 onion, halved
1 clove garlic, halved
2 T. olive oil
2 qts. cold water
4 sprigs fresh parsley
4 sprigs fresh thyme
2 bay leaves
Optional: salt and pepper to taste

Place chicken in an ungreased roasting pan. Cover and roast at 350 degrees for 1-1/2 hours, or until juices run clear when chicken is pierced with a fork. Cool chicken and shred. Reserve pan drippings and bones. Use shredded chicken in your favorite recipe or freeze for later use. Sauté vegetables and garlic in oil in a stockpot over medium heat for 3 minutes. Add reserved bones, pan drippings, water and seasonings; simmer for one hour. Strain broth; season with salt and pepper, if desired.

Cheesy Vegetable Soup

Mary Gage, Wakewood, CA

Fluffy Whole-Wheat Biscuits

These homemade biscuits are scrumptious with a bowl of hot soup or any country-style meal.

Makes one dozen

1 c. all-purpose flour
1 c. whole-wheat flour
4 t. baking powder
1 T. sugar
3/4 t. salt
1/4 c. butter
1 c. milk

Combine flours, baking powder, sugar and salt; mix well. Cut in butter until mixture resembles coarse crumbs. Stir in milk just until moistened. Turn dough out onto a lightly floured surface; knead gently 8 to 10 times. Roll out to 3/4-inch thickness. Cut with a 2-1/2" round biscuit cutter, or cut into squares with a knife. Place biscuits on an ungreased baking sheet. Bake at 450 degrees for 10 to 12 minutes, until lightly golden. Serve warm.

Mary Ann Johnson, Sycamore, IL

Herbed Cheese Focaccia

Even tastier made with fresh herbs! Substitute one tablespoon of fresh herbs for each teaspoon of dried herbs.

Makes 12 to 14 servings

13.8-oz. tube refrigerated
   pizza dough
1 onion, finely chopped
2 cloves garlic, minced
2 T. olive oil
1 t. dried basil
1 t. dried oregano
1/2 t. dried rosemary
1 c. shredded mozzarella cheese

Unroll dough on a greased baking sheet. Press with fingers to form indentations; set aside. Sauté onion and garlic in oil in a skillet; remove from heat. Stir in herbs; spread mixture evenly over dough. Sprinkle with cheese. Bake at 400 degrees for 10 to 15 minutes, until golden. Slice into squares.

★ SIMPLE SWAP ★ A simple substitution for herbs...use one tablespoon fresh chopped herbs in place of one teaspoon dried herbs.

Fluffy Whole-Wheat Biscuits

Michelle Collins, San Diego, CA

Collins' Best Lentil Soup

Thanks to the hearty ingredients this soup offers, appetites are sure to be well satisfied.

Makes about 10 cups

1 c. dried lentils, rinsed and sorted
14-oz. pkg. turkey Kielbasa, sliced
   1/2-inch thick
6 c. beef broth
1 c. onion, chopped
1 c. celery, chopped
1 c. carrots, peeled and chopped
1 c. redskin potato, diced
2 T. fresh flat-leaf parsley, chopped
1/2 t. pepper
1/8 t. ground nutmeg

Combine all ingredients in a 3-quart slow cooker. Cover and cook on high setting for one hour. Reduce heat to low setting and cook 3 hours. Stir before serving.

Diane Hixon, Niceville, FL

Slow-Cooked Campfire Stew

I used to have a small cafe and one day I made this stew to serve. It was a big hit...even folks who said they didn't like corn or butter beans enjoyed it!

Serves 6 to 8

3 potatoes, peeled and diced
1 onion, chopped
2 16-oz. cans stewed tomatoes
16-oz. can butter beans
16-oz. can creamed corn
14-1/2 oz. container shredded BBQ
   beef
14-1/2 oz. container shredded BBQ
   pork
1 T. Worcestershire sauce
1 T. lemon juice
salt and pepper to taste

In a saucepan, cover potatoes and onion with water. Cook over medium-high heat for 10 to 15 minutes, until tender. Drain, reserving 1/4 cup cooking liquid. Add potatoes, onion and reserved liquid to a slow cooker along with undrained canned vegetables and remaining ingredients. Stir well; cover and cook on low setting for 4 hours.

Collins' Best Lentil Soup

Casii Dodd, Frederick, MD

Cheddar-Chive Muffins

Warm, cheesy muffins with fresh chives make a fitting accompaniment to a steaming bowl of chili or soup.

Makes about one dozen

1 c. all-purpose flour
1/2 c. yellow cornmeal
1 T. baking powder
1 T. sugar
1/2 t. salt
1 egg, beaten
3/4 c. milk
1/2 c. shredded sharp Cheddar
   cheese
1 T. fresh chives, chopped
1 T. butter, melted

Combine flour, cornmeal, baking powder, sugar and salt in a large bowl; mix well and make a well in center of mixture. In a separate bowl, stir together remaining ingredients. Add to flour mixture, stirring just until moistened. Spoon batter into greased muffin cups, filling 2/3 full. Bake at 400 degrees for 18 minutes, or until a toothpick inserted in center comes out clean. Immediately remove muffins from pans. Serve warm.

Jennie Gist, Gooseberry Patch

Lemon Tea Bread

Make this bread a day ahead to allow time for the flavors to blend.

Makes one loaf

1 c. sour cream
3/4 c. sugar
1/2 c. butter, softened
2 eggs, beaten
1 T. poppy seed
1 T. lemon zest
2 T. lemon juice
2 c. all-purpose flour
1 t. baking powder
1 t. baking soda

Combine sour cream, sugar and butter in a large bowl; mix until fluffy. Add eggs, poppy seed, lemon zest and lemon juice; mix well. Combine flour, baking powder and baking soda in a separate bowl; mix well. Add flour mixture to egg mixture and stir well. Spoon batter into a greased 9"x5" loaf pan. Bake at 325 degrees for one hour, or until a toothpick inserted near the center comes out clean. Cool before slicing.

★ SAVE IT! ★ Don't toss that lemon half after it's been juiced! Wrap it and store in the freezer, ready to grate whenever a recipe calls for fresh lemon zest.

Cheddar-Chive Muffins

Lori Vincent, Alpine, UT

Mother's Pull-Apart Cheese Bread

My mother always made this cheese bread for family get-togethers. Although she is no longer with us, I reach for this buttery, savory bread whenever I need to feel closer to her.

Makes 10 to 12 servings

1 unsliced loaf white bakery bread
8-oz. pkg. shredded pasteurized
   process cheese spread
1/2 c. butter, softened and divided
1-1/2 t. onion, finely chopped
1 t. Worcestershire sauce
1/4 t. celery seed

Trim crust off top and sides of loaf with a long serrated knife. Cut loaf into 1-1/2 inch slices without cutting through bottom crust. Cut across slices from end to end, forming 1-1/2 inch squares. Combine cheese, 1/4 cup butter, onion, sauce and celery seed; spread between squares. Melt remaining butter; brush over top and sides of loaf. Place on an ungreased baking sheet. Bake at 350 degrees for 20 to 25 minutes, until hot and golden.

Ursula Juarez-Wall, Dumfries, VA

Delicious Quick Rolls

My Grandma Bohannon was the most amazing woman I know! Not a single holiday meal passed without Grandma's piping-hot rolls. We make them other times of year now because they are so easy to make.

Makes one dozen

1 c. water
1 env. active dry yeast
2 T. sugar
2 T. shortening, melted
1 egg, beaten
2-1/4 c. all-purpose flour
1 t. salt

Heat water until very warm, about 110 to 115 degrees. In a large bowl, dissolve yeast in warm water. Add remaining ingredients; beat until smooth. Cover and let rise until double in size, about 30 to 60 minutes. Punch down. Form dough into 12 balls and place in a greased muffin pan. Cover and let rise again until double, about 30 minutes. Bake at 350 degrees for 15 minutes, or until golden.

★ QUICK ROLLS ★ Turn refrigerated dinner rolls into a pull-apart treat at dinnertime. Cut rolls into 4 wedges and place them in a plastic zipping bag with cheese and some zesty seasonings. Shake 'em up, pile into a greased casserole dish and bake as usual.

Mother's Pull-Apart Cheese Bread

Evelyn Belcher, Monroeton, PA

Grandma's Chicken Noodle Soup

My daughter gave me this recipe years ago...now it's my favorite!

Makes 8 servings

16-oz. pkg. thin egg noodles,
  uncooked
1 t. oil
12 c. chicken broth
1-1/2 t. salt
1 t. poultry seasoning
1 c. celery, chopped
1 c. onion, chopped
Optional: 1 c. carrot, peeled
  and chopped
1/3 c. cornstarch
1/4 c. cold water
4 c. cooked chicken, diced

Cook noodles according to package directions; drain, toss with oil and set aside. In the same pot, combine chicken broth and seasonings; bring to a boil over medium heat. Stir in vegetables; reduce heat to medium-low. Cover and simmer for 15 minutes. Combine cornstarch with cold water in a small bowl; gradually add to soup, stirring constantly. Stir in chicken and noodles; heat through, about 5 to 10 minutes.

Marian Forck, Chamois, MO

Creamy Chicken & Macaroni Soup

A friend made this soup and let me sample it...I loved it! It is a filling soup and great with homemade bread.

Makes 8 servings

2 c. cooked chicken, chopped
16-oz. pkg. frozen mixed vegetables
2 c. chicken broth
10-3/4 oz. can cream of chicken soup
3/4 c. celery, chopped
2 T. dried parsley, or to taste
2 cubes chicken bouillon
20-oz. pkg. frozen macaroni &
  cheese dinner

Combine all ingredients except macaroni & cheese dinner in a slow cooker. Cover and cook on low setting for 4 hours. Add frozen macaroni & cheese. Cover and cook for an additional 2 hours on low setting, stirring occasionally.

★ USE THEM UP! ★ Don't throw away roast chicken bones...use them to make flavorful chicken broth! Cover bones with water in a stockpot. Onion, carrot and celery trimmings can be added too. Simmer gently for 30 to 40 minutes, then strain in a colander. Refrigerate or freeze broth in recipe-size containers.

Grandma's Chicken Noodle Soup

Diane Bailey, Red Lion, PA

Tomato-Tortellini Soup

Mamma mia! This is oh-so satisfying and really easy to put together...ready in about 20 minutes.

Serves 8 to 10

1 T. margarine
3 cloves garlic, minced
3 10-1/2 oz. cans chicken broth
8-oz. pkg. cheese-filled tortellini, uncooked
1/4 c. grated Parmesan cheese
salt and pepper to taste
2/3 c. frozen chopped spinach, thawed and drained
14-1/2 oz. can Italian stewed tomatoes
1/2 c. tomato sauce

Melt margarine in a saucepan over medium heat; add garlic. Sauté for 2 minutes; stir in broth and tortellini. Bring to a boil; reduce heat. Mix in Parmesan cheese, salt and pepper; simmer until tortellini is tender. Stir in spinach, tomatoes and tomato sauce; simmer for 5 minutes, until heated through.

Andrea Pocreva, San Antonio, TX

White Chicken Chili

This chili recipe feeds a crowd! If you're hosting a smaller group, it is easily halved.

Serves 16 to 20

2 onions, chopped
1 T. olive oil
6 c. chicken broth
6 15-1/2 oz. cans Great Northern beans, drained and rinsed
3 5-oz. cans chicken, drained
2 4-oz. cans diced green chiles
2 t. ground cumin
1 t. garlic powder
1-1/2 t. dried oregano
1/4 t. white pepper
12-oz. container sour cream
3 c. shredded Monterey Jack cheese

In a large stockpot over medium heat, sauté onions in oil until tender. Stir in remaining ingredients except sour cream and cheese. Simmer for 30 minutes, stirring frequently, until heated through. Shortly before serving time, add sour cream and cheese. Stir until cheese is melted.

★ STOCK UP! ★ Keep a few packages of frozen cheese ravioli, tortellini or pierogies tucked in the freezer for easy meal-making anytime. They are perfect for tossing into soups or stews, or topped with your favorite sauce as either a side dish or meatless main.

Tomato-Tortellini Soup

Diane Axtell, Marble Falls, TX

Blueberry Scones

Good for breakfast or for a treat any time of the day! Your family will love these amazing scones.

Makes 8 scones

2 c. all-purpose flour
2 T. sugar
1 T. baking powder
1/2 t. baking soda
1/4 t. salt
1 T. orange zest
1/2 c. very cold, butter, cut into
   1-inch pieces
1 c. dried blueberries
2/3 c. buttermilk

In a large bowl, combine flour, sugar, baking powder, baking soda and salt. Add orange zest and mix well. Using a pastry blender, cut in butter until mixture is crumbly, resembling small peas. Add dried blueberries and buttermilk, stirring until just moistened. Turn dough out onto a lightly floured surface; knead 5 or 6 times. Pat into an 8-inch circle. Cut into 8 wedges. Place one inch apart on a lightly greased baking sheet. Bake at 400 degrees for about 15 minutes, or until golden. Let cool. Drizzle with Orange Frosting Drizzle.

Orange Frosting Drizzle

2 c. powdered sugar
2 T. orange juice
1 T. butter, melted
1 t. orange zest
1/3 c. sugar

Mix all ingredients in a small bowl. until creamy and smooth. Place in a piping tube or a small plastic sandwich bag; cut off corner of bag. Drizzle frosting onto scones.

★ FREEZE THEM! ★ So the produce counter had a wonderful sale and now you wonder what to do with 5 pounds of blueberries. Don't fret...it's easy to freeze fresh berries for later! Simply place the berries in a single layer on a baking sheet, freeze, then store in plastic freezer bags.

Blueberry Scones

Karen Swartz, Woodville, OH

Hearty Meatball Stew

Busy day ahead? Prepare the ingredients for this easy recipe the night before. For a special treat, serve it ladled into individual sourdough bread bowls.

Makes 8 servings

1 lb. new potatoes, cubed
16-oz. pkg. baby carrots
1 onion, sliced
2 4-oz. cans sliced mushrooms, drained
16-oz. pkg. frozen meatballs
12-oz. jar beef gravy
14-1/2 oz. can Italian-seasoned diced tomatoes
3-1/4 c. water
pepper to taste
14-1/2 oz. can corn, drained

In a large slow cooker, layer all ingredients except corn in the order listed. Cover and cook on low setting for 8 to 10 hours. About one hour before serving, stir in corn.

LuAnn Tracy, Aliquippa, PA

Italian Wedding Soup

I got this wonderful recipe from my sister's daughter-in-law. Serve with a tangy salad and bread sticks for a simple meal.

Serves 6 to 8

25 frozen cooked Italian meatballs
6 c. chicken broth
1 c. boneless, skinless chicken breast, chopped
1/2 c. carrot, peeled and diced
1/2 c. celery, diced
1 bunch spinach, torn
garlic salt to taste
1/4 c. grated Parmesan-Romano cheese
1/4 c. ditalini pasta, uncooked
Garnish: additional grated Parmesan-Romano cheese

Combine all ingredients except pasta and garnish in a slow cooker. Cover and cook on low setting for 7 to 8 hours. About 20 minutes before serving, cook pasta according to package directions; drain and stir into slow cooker. Sprinkle servings with a little more cheese.

Hearty Meatball Stew

Irene's Portabella Burgers, Page 144

CHAPTER FOUR

First-Class Sides, Salads & Sandwiches

Confetti Corn & Rice Salad, Page 172

Ranch Chicken Wraps, Page 154

Deanne Corona, Hampton, GA

Tomato Fritters

I have no idea where my grandmother picked up this gem of a recipe...she was using it as a bookmark in one of her cookbooks. The first time I tried it, I fell in love. So here is one of my favorite sides using fresh tomatoes!

Serves 4 to 6

1 c. all-purpose flour
1 t. baking powder
1 t. fresh rosemary, snipped
1/8 t. salt
1/8 t. pepper
1 c. ripe tomatoes, cut into 1/2-inch cubes
2 T. onion or leek, finely chopped
1 T. fresh basil, snipped
1/8 t. Worcestershire sauce
1 egg, beaten
oil for frying
Optional: cheese or jalapeño jelly

In a bowl, combine flour, baking powder, rosemary, salt and pepper. Pat tomatoes dry, add to flour mixture. Add remaining ingredients except egg, oil and optional ingredients; don't mix yet. Add egg and stir everything together. In a large skillet over medium-high heat, heat several inches oil to at least 360 degrees. Drop batter into oil by tablespoonfuls, lightly patting them down a bit into the hot oil. Cook until golden on both sides; drain on paper towels. Serve with cheese or jalapeño jelly, if desired.

Julie Preston, Edwardsville, IL

Mom's Magnificent Meatballs

Whenever we get together, my family & friends ask for these delicious meatballs. We love them on sandwiches, pasta or just as an appetizer. You can't go wrong with easy Magnificent Meatballs!

Makes 10 servings

2 lbs. ground beef
1 lb. ground Italian pork sausage
1/4 c. Italian-seasoned dry bread crumbs
1/2 c. shredded Parmesan cheese
1 egg, beaten
3 T. tomato paste
1 T. dried oregano
1 T. dried basil
2 T. garlic salt
1 t. red pepper flakes
3 c. favorite pasta sauce

In a large bowl, combine all ingredients except pasta sauce. Mix until well combined. Form into golfball-size meatballs; arrange meatballs on a rimmed baking sheet. Bake, uncovered, at 400 degrees for 20 minutes, or until no longer pink in the center. Remove from oven and let stand for 10 minutes. Add pasta sauce to a large saucepan over medium heat. Add meatballs and heat through, stirring occasionally. Serve as desired.

Tomato Fritters

Sandra Sullivan, Aurora, CO

Artichoke Tuna Melt

This is no ordinary tuna sandwich! It's topped with tasty, healthy ingredients, perfect for sharing at get-togethers. It's my favorite sandwich...I predict it will become yours too.

Makes 6 servings

1 loaf French bread, halved
1 T. olive oil
1 clove garlic, halved
3/4 c. mayonnaise
1 T. lemon juice
1 T. Dijon mustard
1/2 t. garlic powder
1/2 t. pepper
2 10-oz. cans white tuna packed in
   water, drained and flaked
14-oz. can artichoke hearts, drained,
   rinsed and chopped
1 c. fresh baby spinach
2 plum tomatoes, sliced
1 c. shredded mozzarella cheese

Place halves of loaf cut-side up on an ungreased baking sheet; brush with olive oil. Broil 4 to 6 inches from heat for 2 to 3 minutes, until golden. Rub cut sides of garlic clove over warm bread; discard garlic. In a large bowl, combine mayonnaise, lemon juice, mustard and seasonings; stir in tuna and artichokes. Arrange spinach over bread; top with tuna mixture, tomatoes and cheese. Broil for one minute longer, or until cheese is melted. Slice and serve.

Amanda Carew, Newfoundland, Canada

Spicy Sweet Potato Fries

Change up the sides you serve by making these sweet potato fries with just a touch of spice. They'll love them!

Serves 4 to 6

2 lbs. sweet potatoes, peeled and cut
   into wedges or strips
3 T. olive oil, divided
1 t. seasoned salt
1 t. ground cumin
1/2 t. chili powder
1/2 t. pepper
Optional: ranch salad dressing

Place sweet potatoes in a plastic zipping bag. Sprinkle with 2 tablespoons oil and seasonings; toss to coat. Drizzle remaining oil over a baking sheet; place sweet potatoes in a single layer on sheet. Bake, uncovered, at 425 degrees for 25 to 35 minutes, turning halfway through cooking time, until sweet potatoes are golden. Serve with salad dressing for dipping if desired.

Artichoke Tuna Melt

Carol Lytle, Columbus, OH

Ham Sandwich Supreme

This easy sandwich is always welcome at potlucks, tailgating parties and other get-togethers. One sandwich will not be enough! A friend shared this recipe with me.

Makes 12 sandwiches

1 doz. brown & serve rolls, split
1/2 lb. sliced deli baked ham
12 slices provolone cheese
1/2 c. butter
2 T. brown sugar, packed
1 T. Worcestershire sauce
1 T. mustard
Optional: 1 T. poppy seed

Assemble 12 sandwiches with rolls, ham and cheese. Arrange sandwiches in a lightly buttered 13"x9" baking pan; set aside. Combine remaining ingredients in a small saucepan over medium heat. Bring to a boil, stirring until brown sugar dissolves; spoon over sandwiches. Bake, uncovered, at 350 degrees for 10 to 30 minutes, until crisp and golden on top.

Jamie Davis, Fremont, CA

Chicken-Cheddar Wraps

This is a great way to use leftover chicken...it'll become a family favorite.

Makes 12 servings

1 c. sour cream
1 c. salsa
2 T. mayonnaise
4 c. cooked chicken, cubed
2 c. shredded Cheddar cheese
1 c. sliced mushrooms
2 c. lettuce, shredded
12 flour tortillas
1 c. guacamole
Garnish: tomato wedges

Combine sour cream, salsa and mayonnaise; add chicken, cheese and mushrooms. Divide lettuce between tortillas; top with 1/4 cup chicken mixture on each tortilla. Spread with guacamole; roll up tortilla. Place tortillas on serving dish; garnish with any remaining guacamole and tomato wedges.

★ HANDY TIP ★ To warm tortillas, stack them between moistened paper towels and microwave on high setting for 20 to 30 seconds...easy!

Ham Sandwich Supreme

Judy Croll, Rowlett, TX

Aunt Judy's Baked Macaroni & Cheese

My family always requests this comforting dish for special holiday gatherings. It is so simple to prepare, and delicious with baked ham or just by itself. There are never any leftovers.

Serves 8 to 10

8-oz. pkg. elbow macaroni, uncooked
2 T. oil
1 T. plus 1 t. salt, divided
1/4 c. butter
1/3 c. all-purpose flour
3 c. milk, warmed
1/2 t. pepper
8-oz. pkg. pasteurized process
   cheese, cubed
1/2 c. shredded Cheddar cheese

Cook macaroni according to package directions, adding oil and one tablespoon salt to cooking water; drain and set aside. Meanwhile, melt butter in a large saucepan over medium heat. Add flour; cook and stir for 3 minutes, or until bubbly. Do not brown. Whisk in warm milk and bring to a boil, stirring constantly. Add remaining salt, pepper and cubed cheese. Stir until cheese is melted; remove from heat. Add cooked macaroni to cheese sauce and stir. Transfer to a buttered 2-quart casserole dish. Bake, uncovered, at 350 degrees for 20 to 30 minutes, until bubbly. Top with shredded cheese; return to oven just until cheese melts.

★ WARM IT UP! ★ A wide-mouthed thermos is terrific for keeping mac & cheese, soup and other warm foods fresh and delicious. To keep the thermos hot until lunchtime, fill it with hot water, then empty it just before adding the piping-hot food.

Aunt Judy's Baked Macaroni & Cheese

Sarah Oravecz, Gooseberry Patch

Bratwurst Pretzel Reubens

We love these sandwiches...fun for an Oktoberfest cookout! Sometimes I'll use my own home-baked soft pretzels, but I've found soft pretzels from the grocery's freezer section are good too.

Makes 4 sandwiches

4 bratwursts, halved lengthwise
4 large soft pretzels, warmed if frozen
spicy brown mustard to taste
4 T. butter, divided
4 T. olive oil, divided
4 slices Muenster cheese
1 c. sauerkraut, well drained
pepper to taste

Grill or pan-fry bratwursts as desired; set aside. Meanwhile, slice pretzels in half horizontally; spread the cut sides with mustard. Working in batches, melt one tablespoon butter with one tablespoon olive oil in a skillet over medium-low heat. Add 2 pretzel halves to skillet, crust-side down. Arrange one to 2 cheese slices on each half. Cook just until cheese is nearly melted. With a spatula, remove pretzel halves to a plate. Top one pretzel half with a bratwurst; spoon on 1/4 cup sauerkraut. Season with pepper. Add pretzel top. Repeat with remaining ingredients.

Christine Gordon, Rapid City, SD

French Bread Pizza Burgers

A quick & easy dinner...kids will love to eat this as much as they'll love helping Mom make it! Change it up any way you like, adding other pizza toppings to your own taste.

Serves 6 to 8

1 loaf French bread, halved lengthwise
15-oz. can pizza sauce
1 lb. ground pork sausage, browned and drained
3-1/2 oz. pkg. sliced pepperoni
8-oz. pkg. shredded mozzarella cheese

Place both halves of loaf on an ungreased baking sheet, cut-sides up. Spread with pizza sauce; top with sausage, pepperoni and cheese. Bake at 350 degrees for 15 minutes or until cheese is melted. Slice to serve.

★ BROWN 'EM! ★ Bratwurst and knockwurst are Geman sausages often braised in dark German beer. Just place the sausages in a pan with enough beer to halfway cover them. Bring the beer to a simmer and cook until it has evaporated. Then continue browning the sausages in the pan, or cook them on a hot grill.

Bratwurst Pretzel Reubens

Susan Jacobs, Vista, CA

Bacon-Cheddar Coleslaw

One 4th of July, I wanted to jazz up my coleslaw. We'd been on a low-carb diet and we liked the coleslaw mix sautéed with bacon, so we gave it a try all chilled together. It's yummy!

Serves 8 to 10

3/4 lb. bacon, cut into 1-inch pieces
1 c. mayonnaise
2 T. Dijon mustard
2 T. white vinegar
1/2 t. salt
1/2 t. pepper
Optional: 1 to 2 T. milk
16-oz. pkg. tri-color shredded
    coleslaw mix
8-oz. pkg. shredded Cheddar cheese,
    divided
1/4 c. green onions, chopped

Cook bacon in a skillet over medium heat until crisp. Using a slotted spoon, remove bacon to a paper towel-lined plate. Set aside 3 tablespoons bacon drippings to cool. In a bowl, combine mayonnaise, mustard, vinegar, salt, pepper and reserved drippings. If too thick, thin with a little milk to a salad dressing consistency; set aside. In a large bowl, toss together coleslaw mix, half of cheese and half of bacon. Pour dressing over coleslaw and toss to coat. Sprinkle with remaining cheese, bacon and onions. Cover and chill for 2 hours before serving.

Emilie Britton, New Bremen, OH

Heavenly Onion Casserole

This is amazingly delicious! A wonderful addition to a meal.

Serves 6 to 8

2 T. butter
3 sweet onions, sliced
1/2 lb. sliced mushrooms
1 c. shredded Swiss cheese
10-3/4 oz. can cream of
    mushroom soup
5-oz. can evaporated milk
2 t. soy sauce
6 to 8 slices French bread
6 to 8 slices Swiss cheese

Melt butter in a large skillet over medium heat. Sauté onions and mushrooms until tender; transfer to a greased 2-quart casserole dish. Sprinkle with shredded cheese; set aside. In a bowl, whisk together soup, milk and soy sauce; spoon over cheese. Top with bread slices; arrange cheese slices over bread. Cover loosely and bake at 375 degrees for 30 minutes. Uncover; bake another 15 minutes. Let stand for 5 minutes before serving.

Bacon-Cheddar Coleslaw

Irene Robinson, Cincinnati, OH

Irene's Portabella Burgers

Scrumptious…I promise you won't miss the meat! Serve this on pretzel buns to bring out the beauty of the mushrooms. If you don't wish to fire up the grill, use a heavy grill skillet on your stovetop. However you make this amazing sandwich, your family will love it and won't believe the wonderful flavor and texture of this meatless sandwich.

Makes 4 servings

4 portabella mushroom caps
1 c. Italian salad dressing
4 pretzel or sourdough buns, split
4 slices Muenster or Gruyère cheese
Garnish: romaine lettuce or arugula

Combine mushrooms and salad dressing in a plastic zipping bag, turning to coat. Chill 30 minutes, turning occasionally. Remove mushrooms, discarding dressing. Grill mushrooms, covered with grill lid, over medium heat for 2 to 3 minutes on each side. Grill buns, cutside down, one minute, or until toasted. Top buns with mushroom, cheese and lettuce or arugula; serve immediately.

Eva Hoyle, Mexico, MO

Best Green Beans Ever

My family likes green bean bundles, which take lots of time to prepare, so I created this recipe. It tastes just like the bundles, but it is so quick & easy.

Serves 6 to 8

5 15-oz. cans whole green beans, drained
1 lb. bacon, crisply cooked and crumbled, or 3/4 c. real bacon bits
2/3 c. brown sugar, packed
1/4 c. butter, melted
1/4 c. low-sodium soy sauce
1-1/2 t. garlic powder

Spread green beans in an ungreased 13"x9" baking pan; sprinkle with bacon and set aside. Whisk together remaining ingredients in a bowl; pour over green beans. Bake, uncovered, at 350 degrees for 30 to 40 minutes, until heated through.

★ VEGGIES RULE! ★ For a no-fuss meatless meal, spoon grilled or roasted veggies onto a softened tortilla and roll up…delicious!

Irene's Portabella Burgers

Jolene Koval, Ontario, Canada

Jolene's Chickpea Medley

This unusual meatless salad goes together in a jiffy! The garbanzo beans add protein, texture and amazing flavor. And it is just such a beautiful dish to serve! Add some homemade bread and a favorite cheese and you have a complete meal.

Makes 4 servings

15-oz. can garbanzo beans, drained
    and rinsed
1 red pepper, diced
1 c. kale, finely shredded
1 zucchini, diced
1 ear corn, steamed, kernels cut off,
    or 1/2 c. frozen corn, thawed,
    steamed and cooled
1/2 c. Italian salad dressing

In a salad bowl, combine beans and vegetables. Drizzle with salad dressing; toss to mix. Let stand 15 minutes before serving to allow flavors to blend.

Virginia Shaw, Medon, TN

Mama's Cucumber Salad

I used to take this salad to my sons' baseball award dinners and picnics. Children and adults alike always request this salad...it's cool, refreshing and very simple to make!

Serves 8 to 10

2 cucumbers, sliced
1 bunch green onions, diced, or 1 red
    onion, sliced and separated into rings
2 to 3 tomatoes, diced
1/2 c. zesty Italian salad dressing

Toss together vegetables in a large bowl; pour salad dressing over all and toss to mix. Cover and refrigerate at least 3 hours to overnight.

★ STOCK UP! ★ For hearty salads in a snap, keep unopened cans and jars of diced tomatoes, black olives, chickpeas and marinated artichokes in the fridge. They'll be chilled and ready to toss with fresh greens or cooked pasta at a moment's notice.

Jolene's Chickpea Medley

Abigail Smith, Worthington, OH

Triple-Take Grilled Cheese

This impressive sandwich is sure to be a hit with the kids!

Makes 4 sandwiches

1 T. oil
8 slices sourdough bread
1/4 c. butter, softened and divided
4 slices American cheese
4 slices Muenster cheese
1/2 c. shredded sharp Cheddar cheese
Optional: 4 slices red onion, 4 slices tomato, 1/4 c. chopped fresh basil

Heat oil in a skillet over medium heat. Spread 2 bread slices with one tablespoon butter; place one slice butter-side down on skillet. Layer one slice American, one slice Muenster and 2 tablespoons Cheddar cheese on bread. If desired, top with an onion slice, a tomato slice and one tablespoon basil. Place second buttered bread slice on top of sandwich in skillet. Reduce heat to medium-low. Cook until golden on one side, about 3 to 5 minutes; flip and cook until golden on the other side. Repeat with remaining ingredients.

★ PERFECT PAIR! ★ **Grilled cheese and tomato soup...is there anything more comforting? For delicious soup in a jiffy, heat together a can of condensed tomato soup and a can of diced tomatoes until hot. Stir in a little cream...yum!**

Triple-Take Grilled Cheese

Olivia Gust, Woodburn, OR

Chicken & Wild Rice Soup

This soup is great on a cold winter's day, served with homemade bread right out of the oven.

Makes 6 servings

6 c. water
6-oz. pkg. long-grain and wild
   rice mix
2-oz. pkg. chicken noodle soup mix
2 stalks celery, sliced
1 carrot, peeled and chopped
1/2 c. onion, chopped
2 10-3/4 oz. cans cream of
   chicken soup
2 c. cooked chicken, chopped
salt and pepper to taste

Bring water to a boil in a large stockpot over medium-high heat. Stir in rice mix with seasoning packet and noodle soup mix. Bring to a boil. Cover and simmer over medium-low heat for 10 minutes, stirring occasionally. Add celery, carrot and onion. Cover and simmer 10 minutes, stirring occasionally. Mix in soup, chicken, salt and pepper. Cover and simmer 10 minutes more, stirring occasionally, until rice and vegetables are tender.

April Jacobs, Loveland, CO

The Best-Ever Tomatoes

Enjoy a wonderful fresh-from-the-garden taste by adding these to your favorite chili recipe.

Makes 7, one-quart jars

15 lbs. tomatoes
boiling water
14 T. lemon juice, divided or
   3-1/2 t. citric acid, divided
7 t. canning salt, divided
7 1-quart canning jars and lids,
   sterilized

Dip tomatoes into boiling water until skins split, about 30 to 60 seconds; plunge under cold water and peel. Core; cut into half, if desired. Set aside. Add 2 tablespoons lemon juice or 1/2 teaspoon citric acid to each jar; add tomatoes. Cover with hot water, leaving 1/2-inch headspace; add one teaspoon salt to each jar. Remove air bubbles; secure lids. Process in a boiling water bath for 45 minutes; set jars on a towel to cool. Check for seals.

Chicken & Wild Rice Soup

Jill Burton, Gooseberry Patch

Mexican Chicken & Avocado Salad

Sometimes I serve this over a bed of lettuce, and sometimes over a cup of chilled rice flavored with a squeeze of lime juice. So fresh tasting!

Serves 4 to 6

2 c. deli roast chicken, boned and
　shredded
15-oz. can black beans, drained
　and rinsed
15-oz. can shoepeg corn, drained
1 avocado, halved, pitted and diced
6 green onions, thinly sliced
2 c. tomatoes, chopped, or grape
　tomatoes, halved
Optional: 1/2 c. chopped fresh
　cilantro
1/2 c. citrus vinaigrette salad
　dressing
salt and pepper to taste

In a large bowl, combine chicken, beans, corn, avocado, onions, tomatoes and cilantro, if using. Pour vinaigrette over salad; add salt and pepper to taste. Stir salad to coat vegetables with dressing; cover and chill until serving.

Lisa Seckora, Bloomer, WI

Pasta Taco Salad

Great at potlucks and family gatherings...everyone loves this salad with a kick!

Serves 12 to 14

3 c. rotini pasta, uncooked
1 lb. ground beef
1-1/4 oz. pkg. taco seasoning mix
3/4 c. water
7 c. lettuce, torn
2 tomatoes, chopped
8-oz. pkg. shredded Cheddar cheese
2 c. nacho-flavored tortilla chips,
　crushed

Cook pasta according to package directions; drain and rinse with cold water. Meanwhile, brown beef in a skillet over medium heat; drain. Add taco seasoning and water; cook and stir until thickened. In a large bowl, combine pasta, beef and Dressing; toss until coated. Add lettuce, tomatoes and cheese; toss to combine. Sprinkle with tortilla chips.

Dressing:

1-1/4 c. mayonnaise
3 T. milk
3-3/4 t. sugar
3-3/4 t. cider vinegar
1 T. dry mustard

Whisk together all ingredients.

Mexican Chicken & Avocado Salad

Lea Ann Burwell, Charles Town, WV

Ranch Chicken Wraps

My husband and children just love these easy-to-make wraps and request them often.

Makes 8 to 10 wraps

1/2 t. oil
4 boneless, skinless chicken
   breasts, cut into strips
2.8-oz. can French fried onions
1/4 c. bacon bits
8-oz. pkg. shredded Cheddar cheese
1 bunch leaf lettuce, separated
8 to 10 8-inch flour tortillas
Garnish: ranch salad dressing

Heat oil in a large non-stick skillet over medium heat; add chicken. Cook until chicken is golden and juices run clear when pierced. Add onions, bacon bits and cheese to skillet; cook over low heat until cheese melts. Place several lettuce leaves on each tortilla and spoon chicken mixture down the center; roll up. Serve with ranch salad dressing.

Janice Pigga, Bethlehem, PA

Red Pepper & Chicken Bagels

This is a quick recipe that's perfect whenever time is short.

Makes 2 servings

2 boneless, skinless chicken breasts
1/8 t. salt
1/8 t. pepper
1/4 c. balsamic vinegar
3 T. Worcestershire sauce
2 bagels, split
2 slices fresh mozzarella cheese
2 slices roasted red pepper

Place chicken between 2 pieces of wax paper; pound until thin. Sprinkle with salt and pepper. In a bowl, combine vinegar and Worcestershire sauce; add chicken and marinate for 10 to 15 minutes. Drain and discard marinade. Place chicken on a lightly greased grill or in a skillet over medium heat. Cook and turn until chicken is golden and juices run clear, about 20 minutes. Place chicken on 2 bagel halves; top with cheese and pepper slices. Add remaining bagel halves. Arrange sandwiches on an ungreased baking sheet. Bake at 350 degrees until cheese is melted, about 5 to 10 minutes.

Ranch Chicken Wraps

Molly Cool, Delaware, OH

Bacon-Stuffed Burgers

These go so fast that I have to double the recipe!

Makes 8 sandwiches

4 slices bacon
1/4 c. onion, chopped
4-oz. can mushroom pieces,
    drained and diced
1 lb. ground beef
1 lb. ground pork sausage
1/4 c. grated Parmesan cheese
1/2 t. pepper
1/2 t. garlic powder
2 T. steak sauce
8 sandwich buns, split
Optional: lettuce leaves, tomato
    slices, provolone cheese slices

In a skillet over medium heat, cook bacon until crisp. Remove bacon to a plate, reserving 2 tablespoons drippings in skillet. Add onion to drippings and sauté until tender. Add crumbled bacon and mushrooms; heat through and set aside. Combine beef, sausage, Parmesan cheese, pepper, garlic powder and steak sauce in a large bowl. Mix well and shape into 16 patties. Spoon bacon mixture over 8 patties. Place remaining patties on top and press edges tightly to seal. Grill over medium coals to desired doneness. Serve on buns with lettuce, tomato and cheese, if desired.

★ SAVVY SIDE ★ A tasty apple coleslaw goes well with Bacon-Stuffed Burgers. Simply toss together a large bag of coleslaw mix and a chopped Granny Smith apple. Stir in coleslaw dressing or mayonnaise to desired consistency.

Bacon-Stuffed Burgers

Pamela Forrester, Pontoon Beach, IL

Best-Ever Spinach Salad

Everyone loves this salad, even kids and people who say they don't like spinach!

Serves 8 to 10

1 bunch fresh spinach, torn
6 eggs, hard-boiled, peeled and
    sliced
1 lb. bacon, crisply cooked and
    crumbled
1/2 c. olive oil
1/4 c. sugar
2 T. cider vinegar
1/2 t. salt
1/4 t. dry mustard
Optional: 1 T. dried, minced onion

In a large bowl, combine spinach, eggs and bacon. In a separate bowl, whisk together remaining ingredients. Before serving, drizzle dressing over spinach mixture and toss lightly to coat.

Amanda Lusignolo, Columbus, OH

Tarragon Steak Dinner Salad

Delicious...a perfect light summer meal.

Makes 4 servings

6 c. Boston lettuce
2 pears, peeled, cored and sliced
1/2 red onion, thinly sliced
1/2 lb. grilled beef steak, thinly
    sliced
1/4 c. crumbled blue cheese
1/2 c. red wine vinaigrette salad
    dressing
1 T. fresh tarragon, minced
1/4 t. pepper

Arrange lettuce, pears and onion on 4 serving plates. Top with sliced steak and sprinkle with cheese. Combine dressing, tarragon and pepper in a small bowl; whisk well. Drizzle dressing mixture over salad.

★ EASY EGGS! ★ Hard-boiled eggs made easy! Cover eggs with an inch of water in a saucepan and place over medium-high heat. As soon as the water boils, cover the pan and remove from heat. Let stand for 18 to 20 minutes...cover with ice water, peel and they're done.

Best-Ever Spinach Salad

Kathy Milligan, Mira Loma, CA

Sesame-Asparagus Salad

Our family loves this salad in springtime when asparagus is fresh...it tastes terrific and is easy to prepare.

Makes 4 to 6 servings

1-1/2 lbs. asparagus, cut diagonally
  into 2-inch pieces
3 T. toasted sesame oil
1 t. white wine vinegar
4 t. soy sauce
2-1/2 T. sugar or honey
4 t. toasted sesame seed

Bring a large saucepan of water to a boil over high heat. Add asparagus; cook for 2 to 3 minutes, just until crisp-tender. Immediately drain asparagus; rinse with cold water until asparagus is completely cooled. Drain again; pat dry. Cover and refrigerate until chilled, about one hour. In a small bowl, whisk together remaining ingredients; cover and refrigerate. At serving time, drizzle asparagus with dressing; toss to coat.

Julie Horn, Chrisney, IN

Texas Steak Sandwiches

The family will love this thick-toasted sandwich!

Makes 4 sandwiches

8 slices frozen Texas toast
1-1/2 lbs. deli roast beef, sliced
steak sauce to taste
8 slices provolone cheese
Optional: sliced green pepper and
  red onion, sautéed

Bake Texas toast on a baking sheet at 425 degrees for about 5 minutes per side, until softened and lightly golden; set aside. Warm roast beef in a skillet over medium heat until most of the juices have evaporated; stir in steak sauce. Divide beef evenly among 4 toast slices; top with cheese, pepper and onion, if desired. Place beef-topped toast and remaining toast on a baking sheet; bake at 425 degrees until cheese is melted. Combine to form sandwiches.

★ HANDY TIP! ★ **Hold the asparagus by both ends and snap off the woody stems...they'll naturally break right where they should!**

Sesame-Asparagus Salad

Sandy Carpenter, Washington, WV

Scrumptious Chicken Sandwiches

These taste so much like a popular restaurant's sandwiches, but cost much less!

Serves 8 to 10

1 egg, beaten
1 c. milk
4 to 6 boneless, skinless chicken
   breasts
1 c. all-purpose flour
2-1/2 T. powdered sugar
1 T. kosher salt
1/2 t. pepper
Optional: 1/8 t. allspice
oil for frying
4 to 6 hamburger buns, split and
   lightly toasted
Garnish: mayonnaise, dill pickle
   slices

Mix egg and milk together in an 11"x7" baking pan. Place chicken in pan, turn to coat and refrigerate for one hour. In a bowl, combine flour, sugar and spices. In a heavy skillet, heat one inch of oil to 400 degrees. Working in batches of 3, drain chicken, reserving egg mixture, and lightly dredge in flour mixture. Dip back into egg mixture, then into flour mixture again. Place very carefully into hot oil. Fry for 8 to 10 minutes, until done on both sides and juices run clear. Drain chicken on a wire rack. Assemble sandwiches on toasted buns and garnish as desired.

★ TIME-SAVER ★ Lots of recipes start with cooked chicken breasts. Save time and money... buy chicken in bulk and roast or simmer it all at once. When cooled, pack recipe-size portions of chicken in freezer bags and freeze. They'll thaw quickly when you're ready to use them.

Scrumptious Chicken Sandwiches

Susan Brees, Lincoln, NE

Tuna Seashell Salad

I took this yummy salad to a potluck party and it won 1st place!

Serves 6 to 8

16-oz. pkg. shell macaroni,
    uncooked
12-oz. can tuna, drained
3 eggs, hard-boiled, peeled and diced
4-oz. pkg. mild Cheddar cheese,
    diced
1/2 to 1 c. mayonnaise-type salad
    dressing
1/4 c. sweet pickle relish

Cook macaroni according to package directions; drain. Rinse macaroni with cold water; drain well. Combine all ingredients in a large serving bowl; chill.

Francie Stutzman, Dalton, OH

Chicken & Rice Salad

This dish is scrumptious...I hope you'll try it!

Makes 4 servings

3 T. red wine vinegar
1-1/2 T. extra-virgin olive oil
1/4 t. pepper
1 clove garlic, minced
2 c. long-grain rice, cooked
1-1/2 c. cooked chicken breast, diced
1/2 c. jarred roasted red peppers,
    drained and diced
1/2 c. Kalamata olives, halved
    and pitted
1/4 c. fresh chives, chopped
1/4 c. fresh basil, chopped
1/4 c. fresh oregano, chopped
14-oz. can artichokes, drained
    and diced
4-oz. pkg. crumbled feta cheese

In a small bowl, whisk together vinegar, olive oil, pepper and garlic; set aside. In a separate bowl, combine rice and remaining ingredients except cheese. At serving time, drizzle vinegar mixture over salad; sprinkle with cheese.

Tuna Seashell Salad

J.J. Presley, Portland, TX

Grandma's Buttery Mashed Potatoes

Grandma used to make these mashed potatoes every Sunday for lunch, no matter what the main course was. I can still taste them to this day!

Serves 8 to 12

6 to 8 potatoes, peeled and cubed
1/2 c. butter, softened
1 c. evaporated milk
salt and pepper to taste
Garnish: additional butter,
    fresh chives

Cover potatoes with water in a large saucepan; bring to a boil over medium-high heat. Cook until tender, about 15 minutes; drain. Add remaining ingredients. Beat with an electric mixer on medium speed until blended and creamy. Garnish as desired.

Shellye McDaniel, Texarkana, TX

The Best-Ever Potato Salad

A homestyle potato salad that's just plain good!

Serves 6 to 8

4 c. potatoes, peeled, cubed and
    boiled
4 eggs, hard-boiled, peeled and
    chopped
1 c. mayonnaise
1-1/2 c. celery, chopped
1/2 c. green onions, chopped
1/4 c. radishes, chopped
2 T. fresh parsley, chopped
1 T. cider vinegar
2 t. mustard
1/2 t. celery seed
1-1/2 t. salt
1 t. pepper

Combine all ingredients in a large serving bowl; mix well. Cover and refrigerate until serving.

★ GOT LEFTOVERS? ★ Make crispy potato pancakes with extra mashed potatoes. Stir an egg yolk and some minced onion into 2 cups cold mashed potatoes. Form into patties, dust with a little flour and pan-fry in a little oil until golden.

Grandma's Buttery Mashed Potatoes

Liz Plotnick-Snay, Gooseberry Patch

Mandarin Orange Salad

Quick & easy to prepare, this salad is best topped with a sweet dressing like Raspberry Vinaigrette.

Makes 4 servings

4 c. green or red leaf lettuce, torn
    into bite-size pieces
2 15-oz. cans mandarin oranges,
    drained
1/2 c. walnut pieces, toasted
1/2 red onion, sliced

Combine all ingredients. Toss with desired amount of Raspberry Vinaigrette.

Raspberry Vinaigrette:

1/3 c. raspberry vinegar
1/3 c. seedless raspberry jam
1 t. coriander or ground cumin
1/2 t. salt
1/4 t. pepper
3/4 c. olive oil

Combine fi rst 5 ingredients in blender. Turn blender on high; gradually add oil. Chill.

Claudia Olsen, Chester, NJ

Penne & Goat Cheese Salad

One of my husband's favorite pasta salads...it's just a little different from most. Try arugula for a slightly spicy taste, or feta cheese if you prefer it to goat cheese.

Makes 8 servings

12-oz. pkg. penne pasta, uncooked
1 T. garlic, minced
1/4 c. mayonnaise
4-oz. pkg. goat cheese, diced
1/2 c. sun-dried tomatoes packed in
    oil, drained and oil reserved
2 c. baby spinach, coarsely chopped

Cook pasta according to package directions; drain and rinse with cold water. In a large bowl, combine pasta with garlic, mayonnaise and goat cheese. Finely chop tomatoes and add along with spinach; mix gently. Stir in reserved oil from tomatoes, one tablespoon at a time, until ingredients are nicely coated. Serve at room temperature, or cover and chill.

Mandarin Orange Salad

Janice O'Brien, Warrenton, VA

Summery Herbed Tomato Pie

A refrigerated pie crust makes this one quick-to-fix dish.

Serves 8 to 10

9-inch pie crust
3 to 4 tomatoes, sliced
1/2 c. fresh chives, chopped
2 T. fresh basil, chopped
salt and pepper to taste
2 c. shredded mozzarella cheese
1/2 c. mayonnaise
Garnish: additional fresh chives
   and basil, chopped

Press pie crust into a 9" pie plate. Bake at 425 degrees for 5 minutes. Reduce oven to 400 degrees. Arrange tomato slices in crust; sprinkle with chives, basil, salt and pepper. Combine cheese and mayonnaise; spread over tomatoes. Bake at 400 degrees for 35 minutes. Garnish with additional chives and basil.

Heather Quinn, Gilmer, TX

Tomato-Ravioli Soup

This soup has a light, smooth flavor...there's always an empty pot afterwards!

Serves 6 to 8

1 lb. ground beef
28-oz. can crushed tomatoes
6-oz. can tomato paste
2 c. water
1-1/2 c. onion, chopped
2 cloves garlic, minced
1/4 c. fresh parsley, chopped
3/4 t. dried basil
1/2 t. dried oregano
1/4 t. dried thyme
1/2 t. onion salt
1/2 t. salt
1/4 t. pepper
1/2 t. sugar
9-oz. pkg. frozen cheese ravioli,
   uncooked
1/4 c. grated Parmesan cheese

In a Dutch oven, cook beef over medium heat until no longer pink; drain. Stir in tomatoes with juice, tomato paste, water, onion, garlic, seasonings and sugar. Bring to a boil. Reduce heat; cover and simmer for 30 minutes. Meanwhile, cook ravioli as package directs; drain. Add ravioli to soup and heat through. Stir in Parmesan cheese; serve immediately.

Summery Herbed Tomato Pie

Lois Carswell, Kennesaw, GA

Confetti Corn & Rice Salad

This colorful salad is a favorite at our family gatherings and barbecues, especially during the summer when we can use fresh-picked sweet corn...yum!

Makes 8 servings

4 ears corn, husked
1-1/2 c. cooked rice
1 red onion, thinly sliced
1 green pepper, halved and thinly sliced
1 pt. cherry tomatoes, halved
Optional: 1 jalapeño pepper, thinly sliced

With a sharp knife, cut corn from cob in "planks." In a serving bowl, combine rice, red onion, green pepper, tomatoes and jalapeño pepper, if using. Mix in corn, keeping some corn planks for top. Drizzle with Simple Dressing. Serve at room temperature or refrigerate overnight before serving.

Simple Dressing:

2 T. red wine vinegar
2 T. olive oil
salt and pepper to taste

Whisk all ingredients together.

Teresa Willett, Ontario, Canada

Grilled Chicken & Zucchini Wraps

These wraps are a huge hit with my family...even my son who claims he doesn't like zucchini!

Makes 8 servings

4 boneless, skinless chicken breasts
4 to 6 zucchini, sliced lengthwise into 1/4-inch thick slices
1 to 2 T. olive oil
salt and pepper to taste
1/2 c. ranch salad dressing, divided
8 10-inch whole-grain flour tortillas
8 leaves lettuce
Garnish: shredded Cheddar cheese

Brush chicken and zucchini with olive oil; sprinkle with salt and pepper. Grill chicken over medium-high heat for 5 minutes. Turn chicken over; add zucchini to grill. Grill 5 minutes longer, or until chicken juices run clear and zucchini is tender. Slice chicken into strips; set aside. For each wrap, spread one tablespoon salad dressing on a tortilla. Top with a lettuce leaf, 1/2 cup chicken and 3 to 4 slices of zucchini. Sprinkle with cheese; roll up.

Confetti Corn & Rice Salad

Cris Goode, Mooresville, IN

Grilled Bacon Corn on the Cob

The bacon flavors the corn... delicious!

Makes 6 servings

6 ears sweet corn, husked
1/4 c. butter, softened
salt and pepper to taste
6 slices bacon

Coat each ear of corn with 2 teaspoons butter; season with salt and pepper. Wrap a slice of bacon around each ear. Wrap each ear loosely in heavy-duty aluminum foil. Place corn on a grill over medium heat. Cook for about 30 minutes, turning frequently, until bacon is crisp. Unwrap carefully to serve.

Brandi Glenn, Los Osos, CA

Gobblin' Good Turkey Burgers

This was my mom's recipe...I'll take these over plain old hamburgers any day!

Makes 4 to 6 sandwiches

1 lb. ground turkey
1 onion, minced
1 c. shredded Cheddar cheese
1/4 c. Worcestershire sauce
1/2 t. dry mustard
salt and pepper to taste
6 to 8 hamburger buns, split

Combine all ingredients except buns; form into 4 to 6 patties. Grill to desired doneness; serve on hamburger buns.

★ MIX IT UP! ★ **Make herb butter for corn on the cob by mixing butter in a food processor with fresh chopped chives, dill or thyme. Delicious!**

Grilled Bacon Corn on the Cob

Janine Kuras, Warren, MI

Cheesy Spinach Pie

Two cheeses combine to make this dish delectable.

Makes 8 servings

2 c. cottage cheese
2/3 c. crumbled feta cheese
1/4 t. pepper
10-oz. pkg. frozen chopped spinach,
   thawed and drained
3 eggs, beaten
1/4 c. butter, melted
2 T. all-purpose flour
2 t. dried, minced onion

In a large bowl, combine ingredients in order listed; mix well. Spread in a greased 1-1/2 quart casserole dish. Bake, uncovered, at 350 degrees for 45 minutes, or until center is set.

Deborah Lomax, Peoria, IL

Sunflower Strawberry Salad

A great chilled salad...super for hot summer days!

Makes 6 servings

2 c. strawberries, hulled and sliced
1 apple, cored and diced
1 c. seedless green grapes, halved
1/2 c. celery, thinly sliced
1/4 c. raisins
1/2 c. strawberry yogurt
2 T. sunflower kernels
Optional: lettuce leaves

In a large bowl, combine fruit, celery and raisins. Stir in yogurt. Cover and chill one hour. Sprinkle with sunflower kernels just before serving. Spoon over lettuce leaves, if desired.

★ FREEZE IT! ★ Make your own cooked frozen spinach...it's easy! Just blanch a small bunch of spinach in boiling water for 2 minutes, then remove to a bowl of ice water. Drain well, and freeze in freezer zip-top bags until ready to use.

Cheesy Spinach Pie

Bar-B-Q Chicken Veggie Stir-Fry, Page 182

CHAPTER FIVE

Splendid Savory Suppers

Beef Fajita Skewers, Page 196

Deb's Garden Bounty Dinner, Page 206

Linda Peterson, Mason, MI

Turkey, Black Bean & Sweet Potato Tacos

Bored with the same ol' tacos? These are packed with delicious fresh ingredients! Any leftover filling can be frozen for another meal.

Serves 8 to 10

1 lb. ground turkey
2 T. taco seasoning mix
1/2 c. tomato sauce
15-oz. can black beans, drained and rinsed
3 sweet potatoes, peeled and diced
2 T. butter, sliced
1-1/2 c. fresh spinach, chopped
1-1/2 c. shredded Cheddar cheese
8 to 10 corn taco shells
Garnish: sour cream, salsa, guacamole

Brown turkey in a skillet over medium-high heat; drain. Stir in taco seasoning, tomato sauce and beans; set aside. In a lightly greased 13"x9" baking pan, layer as follows: sweet potatoes, sliced butter, spinach, turkey mixture and cheese. Cover with aluminum foil. Bake at 375 degrees for 45 minutes, or until sweet potatoes are tender. Serve spooned into taco shells, garnished as desired.

Lauren Williams, Kewanee, MO

Easy Enchilada Casserole

We love this casserole...it combines so many textures and flavors! Top it with sour cream and salsa for a southwestern-style feast.

Makes 8 servings

2 lbs. ground beef
1 onion, chopped
10-oz. can enchilada sauce
10-3/4 oz. can cream of mushroom soup
10-3/4 oz. can cream of chicken soup
16-oz. pkg. shredded Cheddar cheese
6-oz. pkg. corn chips

In a large skillet over medium heat, brown beef and onion; drain well. Stir in sauce and soups. Transfer beef mixture to a lightly greased 13"x9" baking pan; top with cheese and corn chips. Bake, uncovered, at 350 degrees for 45 minutes, or until hot and bubbly.

★ KEEP IT FRESH! ★ A refrigerator's vegetable drawer is designed to keep fruits and veggies fresh and tasty. There are just a few exceptions...sweet potatoes, potatoes, onions and hard-shelled squash should be stored in a bin at room temperature.

Turkey, Black Bean & Sweet Potato Tacos

Audrey Kleespies, Alexandria, MN

Bar-B-Q Chicken Veggie Stir-Fry

You can eat a plate full of this yummy recipe with no guilt! Serve on a pretty plate with a bread stick on the side, if you like. It has a bite from the barbecue sauce and is delicious!

Serves 3 to 4

3/4 c. cooked chicken, cubed
1 T. spicy barbecue sauce
1 T. safflower or olive oil
Optional: 1 T. onion, minced
2 zucchini, sliced
2 yellow squash, sliced
3/4 c. carrot, peeled and shredded
12 sugar peas or snow pea pods, coarsely chopped
Optional: sliced almonds to taste

Toss chicken cubes with barbecue sauce; set aside. In a large skillet, heat oil over medium-high heat. Add onion, if using; cook until golden. Add remaining vegetables and chicken mixture. Cook for several minutes, using a spatula to flip, until mixture is dark golden on the edges but vegetables remain tender-crisp. Top with almonds.

Jo Ann, Gooseberry Patch

Chicken Lasagna with Roasted Red Pepper Sauce

There's nothing like a hot pan of lasagna on a cold winter's night! The Roasted Red Pepper Sauce is also great over your favorite noodles.

Serves 6 to 8

4 c. cooked chicken, finely chopped
2 8-oz. containers chive & onion cream cheese
10-oz. pkg. frozen chopped spinach, thawed and well drained
1 t. seasoned pepper
3/4 t. garlic salt
9 no-boil lasagna noodles, uncooked
8-oz. pkg. shredded Italian 3-cheese blend

Stir together chicken, cream cheese, spinach and seasonings; set aside. Layer a lightly greased 11"x7" baking pan with 1/3 of Roasted Red Pepper Sauce, 3 noodles, 1/3 of chicken mixture and 1/3 of cheese. Repeat layers twice. Place baking pan on a baking sheet. Bake, covered, at 350 degrees for 50 to 55 minutes or until thoroughly heated. Uncover and bake 15 more minutes.

Roasted Red Pepper Sauce:

12-oz. jar roasted red peppers, drained
16-oz. jar creamy Alfredo sauce
3/4 c. grated Parmesan cheese
1/2 t. red pepper flakes

Process all ingredients in a food processor until smooth, stopping to scrape down sides as needed. Makes 3-1/2 cups.

Bar-B-Q Chicken Veggie Stir-Fry

Michelle Greeley, Hayes, VA

Gourmet Beef-Noodle Casserole

Cream cheese and Cheddar cheese make this casserole extra rich and creamy.

Serves 6 to 8

1 lb. ground beef
14-1/2 oz. can diced tomatoes
8-oz. can tomato sauce
1/2 c. green pepper, chopped
4-oz. can sliced mushrooms, drained
1 clove garlic, chopped
2 t. salt
2 t. sugar
1/2 c. Burgundy wine or beef broth
8-oz. pkg. cream cheese, softened
1 c. sour cream
1/3 c. onion, chopped
2 c. shredded Cheddar cheese, divided
8-oz. pkg. wide egg noodles, cooked and divided

Brown ground beef in a skillet over medium-high heat; drain. Add tomatoes with juice, sauce, green pepper, mushrooms, garlic, salt, sugar and wine or broth; cover and simmer over low heat 10 minutes. In a medium bowl, blend cream cheese, sour cream, onion and one cup Cheddar cheese; set aside. In an ungreased 13"x9" baking pan, layer half the beef mixture, half the noodles and half the cream cheese mixture; repeat layers. Top with remaining Cheddar cheese. Bake, uncovered, at 350 degrees for 40 minutes.

★ QUICK & EASY ★ Here's an oh-so-easy way to cook up egg noodles: when water comes to a rolling boil, turn off the heat. Add the noodles and cover the pot. Let stand for 20 minutes, stirring once or twice...done!

Gourmet Beef-Noodle Casserole

Beverly Bray, Huber Heights, OH

Roasted Red, Green & Yellow Peppers

These stuffed roasted peppers are as tasty as they are colorful!

Makes 6 servings

2 green peppers
2 red peppers
2 yellow peppers
3 T. olive oil
3 c. green onions, diced
3/4 lb. sliced mushrooms
1 T. fresh thyme, chopped
3/4 c. couscous, uncooked
6 T. water
6 plum tomatoes, chopped

Cut off the top third of each pepper and discard. Remove seeds and rinse peppers well; set aside. Heat oil in a large skillet over medium-high heat. Add onions and mushrooms; sauté for 5 minutes. Add thyme, couscous and water; blend well. Remove from heat and stir in tomatoes. Stuff peppers with couscous mixture and place in a lightly greased 13"x9" baking pan. Bake, uncovered, at 400 degrees for 35 minutes, or until peppers are tender.

Thomas Hiegel, Union City, OH

Tom's Best-Ever Salmon Patties

I decided I wanted to eat more fish and less beef, but didn't want any fishy taste. These tasty patties are what I came up with.

Makes 8 servings

15-1/2 oz. can wild pink salmon, drained
1/2 c. sweet onion, chopped
1/4 c. celery, chopped
2 T. butter, divided
12 saltine crackers, finely crushed
1/4 c. buttermilk
2 eggs, beaten
1 T. lemon juice
1/2 t. white pepper
Optional: 2 T. prepared horseradish

Discard any skin from salmon; add salmon to a large bowl and set aside. In a skillet over medium heat, sauté onion and celery in one tablespoon butter for 4 to 5 minutes, until tender. Add onion mixture and remaining ingredients except butter to salmon in bowl; mix well and shape into 8 patties. Melt remaining butter in same skillet over medium heat; carefully add salmon patties. Cook on both sides until golden.

Roasted Red, Green & Yellow Peppers

Melody Taynor, Everett, WA

Lemony Pork Piccata

Serve over quick-cooking angel hair pasta to enjoy every drop of the lemony sauce.

Makes 4 servings

1-lb. pork tenderloin, sliced into
    8 portions
2 t. lemon-pepper seasoning
3 T. all-purpose flour
2 T. butter, divided
1/4 c. dry sherry or chicken broth
1/4 c. lemon juice
1/4 c. capers
4 to 6 thin slices lemon

Pound pork slices to 1/8-inch thickness, using a meat mallet or rolling pin. Lightly sprinkle pork with seasoning and flour. Melt one tablespoon butter in a large skillet over medium-high heat. Add half of pork and sauté for 2 to 3 minutes on each side, until golden, turning once. Remove pork to a serving plate; set aside. Repeat with remaining butter and pork. Add sherry or chicken broth, lemon juice, capers and lemon slices to skillet. Cook for 2 minutes or until slightly thickened, scraping up browned bits. Add pork and heat through.

Vickie, Gooseberry Patch

Burgundy Meatloaf

A mixture of ground beef and ground pork can also be used.

Serves 6 to 8

2 lbs. ground beef
2 eggs, beaten
1 c. soft bread crumbs
1 onion, chopped
1/2 c. Burgundy wine or beef broth
1/2 c. fresh parsley, chopped
1 T. fresh basil, chopped
1-1/2 t. salt
1/4 t. pepper
5 slices bacon
1 bay leaf
8-oz. can tomato sauce

Combine ground beef, eggs, crumbs, onion, wine or broth, herbs and seasonings in a large bowl; mix well and set aside. Criss-cross 3 bacon slices on a 12-inch square of aluminum foil. Form beef mixture into a 6-inch round loaf on top of bacon. Cut remaining bacon slices in half; arrange on top of meatloaf. Place bay leaf on top. Lift meatloaf by aluminum foil into a slow cooker; cover and cook on high setting for one hour. Reduce heat to low setting and continue cooking, covered, for 4 more hours. Remove meatloaf from slow cooker by lifting foil. Place on a serving platter, discarding foil and bay leaf. Warm tomato sauce and spoon over sliced meatloaf.

Lemony Pork Piccata

Donna Riggins, Albertville, AL

Old-Fashioned Chicken Pot Pie

This makes two savory pies...share one with a neighbor or freeze it to use later.

Makes 2 pies, 6 servings each

4 9-inch frozen pie crusts, thawed
    and divided
5 to 6 boneless, skinless chicken
    breasts, cooked and chopped
1 onion, chopped
10-3/4 oz. can cream of chicken soup
10-3/4 oz. can cream of mushroom
    soup
8-oz. container sour cream
salt and pepper to taste

Line two 9" pie plates with one crust each; set aside. Combine remaining ingredients in a large bowl; mix well. Divide mixture between pie plates; top with remaining crusts. Crimp crusts to seal and cut several slits in top. Bake at 350 degrees for 35 to 45 minutes, until bubbly and crusts are golden.

Judy Davis, Muskogee, OK

Mushroom-Garlic-Chicken Pizza

This recipe gets a big "YUM" at our house...try it! It's a great way to use leftover baked or grilled chicken too.

Serves 6 to 8

12-inch Italian pizza crust
3/4 c. ranch salad dressing
2 T. garlic, minced
1 chicken breast, cooked and sliced
2 4-oz. cans sliced mushrooms,
    drained
salt and pepper to taste
8-oz. pkg. shredded mozzarella
    cheese
Optional: fresh oregano leaves, red
    pepper flakes

Place crust on an ungreased pizza pan or baking sheet. Spread salad dressing and garlic over crust. Arrange sliced chicken and mushrooms on top. Add salt and pepper to taste; cover with cheese. Bake at 400 degrees for 8 to 10 minutes, until cheese melts. Cut into wedges. Garnish with oregano and red pepper, if desired.

Old-Fashioned Chicken Pot Pie

Betty Lou Wright, Hendersonville, TN

Top-Prize Chicken Casserole

This crowd-pleasing dish has graced my family's table for decades. First prepared by my mother-in-law, it's been taken to many potlucks and church suppers. With its creamy sauce and crunchy topping, it's always a hit.

Serves 6 to 8

2 to 3 c. cooked chicken, cubed
2 10-3/4 oz. cans cream of
    mushroom soup
4 eggs, hard-boiled, peeled and
    chopped
1 onion, chopped
2 c. cooked rice
1-1/2 c. celery, chopped
1 c. mayonnaise
2 T. lemon juice
3-oz. pkg. slivered almonds
5-oz. can chow mein noodles

Combine all ingredients except almonds and noodles in a large bowl; mix well. Transfer mixture to a lightly greased 3-quart casserole dish. Cover and refrigerate 8 hours to overnight. Stir in almonds. Bake, uncovered, at 350 degrees for 40 to 45 minutes, until heated through. Top with noodles; bake 5 more minutes.

Dorothy Benson, Baton Rouge, LA

Chicken Spaghetti Deluxe

This recipe is reminiscent of cold winter days and the inviting smells of Mom's warm kitchen. Best of all, the pasta doesn't need to be cooked ahead of time.

Makes 8 servings

2 c. cooked chicken, chopped
8-oz. pkg. spaghetti, uncooked and
    broken into 2-inch pieces
1 c. celery, chopped
1 c. onion, chopped
1 c. yellow pepper, chopped
1 c. red pepper, chopped
2 10-3/4 oz. cans cream of
    mushroom soup
1 c. chicken broth
1/4 t. Cajun seasoning or pepper
1 c. shredded Cheddar cheese

Mix chicken, spaghetti, celery, onion, yellow pepper and red pepper in a bowl. Whisk together soup, broth and seasoning in a separate bowl. Add chicken mixture to soup mixture. Spread chicken mixture in a lightly greased 13"x9" baking pan; sprinkle cheese over top. Cover with aluminum foil coated with non-stick vegetable spray. Bake at 350 degrees for 45 minutes. Uncover and bake for 10 more minutes.

Top-Prize Chicken Casserole

JoAnn, Gooseberry Patch

Mexican Lasagna

Use a colorful tablecloth or runner and napkins in vivid hues to give the table a Mexican flair.

Makes 6 servings

1 lb. ground beef
16-oz. can refried beans
2 t. dried oregano
1 t. ground cumin
3/4 t. garlic powder
2 c. picante sauce
1-1/2 c. water
9 lasagna noodles, uncooked
16-oz. container sour cream
3/4 c. green onions, thinly sliced
2-1/4 oz. can sliced black olives, drained
1 c. shredded Monterey Jack cheese

Brown beef in a large non-stick skillet, stirring until it crumbles; drain and set aside beef. Wipe skillet clean. Return beef to skillet; stir in beans and seasonings. Combine picante sauce and water in a bowl. Pour 1-1/3 cups sauce mixture into a lightly greased 13"x9" baking pan; arrange 3 noodles over sauce mixture. Spread half of beef mixture evenly over noodles; pour one cup remaining sauce mixture over beef mixture and top with 3 more noodles. Spread remaining beef mixture over noodles; top with 3 remaining noodles and spread remaining sauce mixture evenly over noodles. Cover and bake at 350 degrees for 1-1/2 hours. Combine sour cream, onions and olives in a small bowl. Spread sour cream mixture over lasagna and top with cheese. Return to oven and bake 10 more minutes. Let stand 10 minutes before serving.

★ FREEZE IT! ★ Cut baked lasagna into serving portions and freeze on a baking sheet, then pack frozen portions in a freezer bag. Later you'll be able to heat up just the number of servings you need.

Mexican Lasagna

Jerry Lyttle, St. Clair Shores, MI

Beef Fajita Skewers

Serve with warmed flour tortillas, sour cream and salsa...a clever new way to enjoy a Mexican restaurant favorite.

Makes 4 to 6 servings

1 lb. boneless beef top sirloin, sliced
    into 1-inch cubes
8 wooden skewers, soaked in water
1 green pepper, cut into wedges
1 red or yellow pepper, cut into
    wedges
2 onions, cut into wedges
3 T. lime juice
1/3 c. Italian salad dressing
salt to taste

Thread beef cubes onto 4 skewers; thread peppers and onions onto remaining skewers. Combine lime juice and salad dressing; brush over skewers. Grill over hot coals or on a medium-hot grill, turning occasionally, 7 to 9 minutes for beef and 12 to 15 minutes for vegetables. Sprinkle with salt to taste.

Brenda Bodnar, Mayfield Village, OH

Sweet & Spicy Roast Beef

I've been making this for years...the heavenly smell of the slow-simmering beef warms heart & soul and piques the appetite.

Serves 8 to 10

1 onion, sliced and separated
    into rings
3 to 4-lb. bottom-round beef roast
1 T. garlic powder
1 t. pepper
12-oz. can regular or non-alcoholic
    beer
1 c. catsup
1/4 c. brown sugar, packed
3 T. all-purpose flour
1 T. prepared horseradish, or to taste

Add onion rings to a lightly greased slow cooker; set aside. Sprinkle roast on all sides with garlic powder and pepper; add to slow cooker. Combine remaining ingredients in a bowl; mix well and spoon over roast. Cover and cook on low setting for 8 to 10 hours. Remove roast from slow cooker and slice; serve topped with sauce from slow cooker.

Beef Fajita Skewers

Vickie, Gooseberry Patch

Sensational Sirloin Kabobs

Red peppers could also be added for an extra punch of color!

Serves 6 to 8

1/2 c. lemon-lime flavored soda
1/4 c. soy sauce
3 T. brown sugar, packed
3 T. white vinegar
1/2 t. garlic powder
1/2 t. seasoned salt
1/2 t. garlic pepper seasoning
2 lbs. beef sirloin steak, cut into
   1-1/2 inch cubes
2 green peppers, cubed
2 yellow peppers, cubed
1/2 lb. mushrooms, stems removed
1 pt. cherry tomatoes
6 to 8 wooden skewers, soaked in
   water
3 c. cooked rice

Combine soda, soy sauce, brown sugar, vinegar and seasonings in a bowl; mix well and set aside. Place steak cubes in a large plastic zipping bag. Add soda mixture, reserving 1/2 cup for basting; seal bag. Refrigerate beef cubes and reserved soda mixture for 8 hours or overnight. Alternately thread steak, peppers, mushrooms and tomatoes onto skewers. Place on a lightly greased grill over high heat. Grill for 10 minutes, or to desired doneness, basting often with reserved marinade during the last 5 minutes of cooking. Serve skewers over cooked rice.

★ SWEET ENDING! ★ Fruit kabobs are a sweet ending to any meal. Arrange chunks of pineapple and banana, plump strawberries and kiwi slices on skewers. For a creamy dipping sauce, blend together 1/2 cup each of cream cheese and marshmallow creme.

Sensational Sirloin Kabobs

Ramona Storm, Gardner, IL

Easy Chicken & Noodles

This smells so good and warms you up on a cold day. Leftover cooked chicken works great. Add some warm, crusty bread and a citrus salad...dinner is served!

Makes 8 servings

16-oz. pkg. frozen egg noodles,
    uncooked
2 14-1/2 oz. cans chicken broth
2 10-3/4 oz. cans cream of chicken
    soup
1/2 c. onion, finely chopped
1/2 c. carrot, peeled and diced
1/2 c. celery, diced
salt and pepper to taste
2 c. boneless, skinless chicken
    breasts, cooked and cubed

Thaw egg noodles (or run package under warm water) just enough to break apart; set aside. Spray a slow cooker with non-stick vegetable spray. Add remaining ingredients except chicken; blend well. Stir in noodles and chicken. Cover and cook on low setting for 7 to 8 hours, until hot and bubbly.

Kathy Courington, Canton, GA

Simple Ginger Chicken

My daughter's girlfriend says this is the best chicken she has ever had. A friend shared the recipe with me years ago...every time I serve it, it disappears! It really is that simple and that good.

Makes 8 servings

6 to 8 chicken thighs
1/2 to 1 onion, chopped
1 c. low-sodium soy sauce
1 c. water
3 T. ground ginger, or to taste
cooked rice

Combine all ingredients except rice in a Dutch oven. Bring to a boil over medium-high heat; reduce heat to low. Cover and simmer for one hour, or until chicken juices run clear. Check occasionally, adding more water as needed. May also be cooked in a slow cooker on low setting for 6 to 8 hours. Serve over cooked rice.

★ HANDY TIP ★ Ginger comes in several different forms...ground, crystallized and fresh. For best results, use the kind specified in a recipe, but in a pinch, 1/4 teaspoon ground ginger equals one tablespoon sliced fresh ginger root.

Easy Chicken & Noodles

Anne Alesauskas, Minocqua, WI

Cashew Chicken

This is one of the simplest recipes in my recipe box and I think you'll love it! We just love Chinese food... unfortunately, our options aren't great for take-out, so I make my own whenever possible. Using the slow cooker is an added bonus on those days when you're running like mad.

Makes 4 servings

1/2 c. all-purpose flour
1/8 t. pepper
2 lbs. boneless, skinless chicken
   breasts, cubed
2 T. canola oil
1/4 c. soy sauce
2 T. rice wine vinegar
2 T. catsup
1 T. brown sugar, packed
1 clove garlic, minced
1/2 t. fresh ginger, peeled and grated
red pepper flakes to taste
cooked brown rice
Garnish: 1/2 c. cashews

Combine flour and pepper in a plastic zipping bag. Add chicken pieces to bag; toss to coat and set aside. Heat oil in a large skillet over medium-high heat. Cook chicken for about 5 minutes, until golden on all sides but not cooked through. Transfer chicken to a slow cooker; set aside. In a small bowl, combine remaining ingredients except rice and cashews. Pour mixture over chicken, stirring slightly. Cover and cook on low setting for 3 to 4 hours, or on high setting for one to 2 hours, until chicken juices run clear. To serve, spoon chicken mixture over cooked rice; top with cashews.

★ FREEZE IT ★ Nuts, shelled or unshelled, will stay fresher longer if they're stored in the freezer. As an added benefit, unshelled nuts will crack much easier when frozen.

Cashew Chicken

Lisa McClelland, Columbus, OH

Chicken Enchilada Nacho Bowls

I created this recipe for a meal that's quick, yet fancy enough to set before company when unexpected guests come for the evening.

Makes 4 servings

8-oz. pkg. cream cheese, cubed and softened
1 c. milk
14-oz. can chicken broth
2-1/2 t. Dijon mustard
1-1/2 t. fresh dill, chopped
1 c. frozen peas
2 green onions, sliced
12-oz. pkg. smoked salmon, flaked
Optional: chopped fresh chives

In a saucepan over medium-low heat, combine all ingredients except salmon and chives. Cook, stirring often, until cheese is melted and soup is smooth. Stir in salmon; heat through. Sprinkle with chives, if desired.

Cherylann Smith, Efland, NC

Best-Ever Lasagna

This is a quick & easy recipe for homestyle lasagna...just add a tossed salad.

Makes 10 servings

1 lb. lean ground beef, browned and drained
1 t. Italian seasoning
8 lasagna noodles, uncooked and broken into thirds
28-oz. jar spaghetti sauce
1/3 c. water
4-oz. can sliced mushrooms, drained
15-oz. container part-skim ricotta cheese
8-oz. pkg. shredded part-skim mozzarella cheese
Garnish: shredded Parmesan cheese

Combine beef and Italian seasoning; set aside. Arrange half of the lasagna noodles in a slow cooker sprayed with non-stick vegetable spray. Spread half of beef mixture over noodles. Top with half each of remaining ingredients except Parmesan cheese. Repeat layering process. Cover and cook on low setting for 5 hours. Garnish with Parmesan cheese.

Chicken Enchilada Nacho Bowls

Deb Grumbine, Greeley, CO

Deb's Garden Bounty Dinner

I love to make this dish because it is a complete meal in a skillet. My entire family loves it when I serve this for a weeknight dinner.

Makes 6 servings

1 T. oil
6 chicken drumsticks
8 zucchini, chopped
1 lb. mushrooms, chopped
1/2 green pepper, chopped
1/2 red pepper, chopped
1 onion, chopped
2 15-oz. cans stewed tomatoes
2 t. garlic, minced
1 t. turmeric
1/2 t. pepper
2 c. cooked brown rice

Heat oil in a skillet over medium-high heat. Add chicken and cook 20 to 25 minutes, or until golden. Set aside and keep warm. Add remaining ingredients except rice to skillet; cook 5 minutes. Return chicken to skillet and continue to cook until juices run clear. Serve alongside servings of rice.

Jennifer Martineau, Delaware, OH

Gramma's Smothered Swiss Steak

This classic recipe is perfect for any night of the week, but I often serve it for Sunday lunch. I serve it with fresh green beans and roasted potatoes.... what a treat!

Makes 6 servings

1-1/2 lbs. beef round steak, cut into serving-size pieces
1 T. oil
1 small onion, halved and sliced
1 carrot, peeled and shredded
1 c. sliced mushrooms
10-3/4 oz. can cream of chicken soup
8-oz. can tomato sauce

Brown beef in oil in a skillet over medium heat; drain and set aside. Arrange vegetables in a slow cooker; place beef on top. Mix together soup and tomato sauce; pour over beef and vegetables. Cover and cook on low setting for 6 to 8 hours, until beef is tender.

★ FLAVOR BOOST! ★ If a recipe calls for stewed tomatoes, take advantage of Mexican or Italian-style. They already have the seasonings added, so there are fewer ingredients for you to buy and measure!

Deb's Garden Bounty Dinner

Jen Sell, Farmington, MN

Chicken Cordon Bleu

This is a special dish I serve family & friends. It is delicious and beautiful every time.

Makes 4 servings

4 4-oz. boneless, skinless chicken
  breasts
2 slices deli ham, cut in half
2 slices Swiss cheese, cut in half
1 egg, beaten
1/2 c. milk
1/4 c. dry bread crumbs
1/2 t. garlic powder
1 t. dried oregano
2 T. grated Parmesan cheese

Flatten chicken breasts between 2 pieces of wax paper until 1/4-inch thick. Top each piece with a 1/2 slice of ham and cheese; roll up tightly, securing with toothpicks. In a small bowl, beat egg and milk together; set aside. In another bowl, combine bread crumbs, garlic powder, oregano and Parmesan cheese. Dip each chicken bundle in egg mixture, then in bread crumbs. Place on a greased baking sheet; bake at 350 degrees for 45 minutes.

★ MAKE YOUR OWN ★ It's simple to make your own bread crumbs. Save extra bread slices (leftover "heels" are fine) and freeze in a plastic bag. When you have enough, bake the slices in a 250-degree oven until dry and crumbly, then tear into sections and pulse in a food processor or blender.

Chicken Cordon Bleu

Emma Brown, Saskatchewan, Canada

Maple Pork Chops

The sweetness of the maple syrup and saltiness of the soy sauce go so well together. My family can't get enough of these...I usually have to double the recipe!

Makes 4 servings

1/2 c. maple syrup
3 T. soy sauce
2 cloves garlic, minced
4 pork chops

In a bowl, whisk together syrup, soy sauce and garlic; reserve 1/4 cup of mixture. Add pork chops to remaining mixture in bowl. Cover and refrigerate for at least 15 minutes to overnight. Drain, discarding mixture in bowl. Grill over medium-high heat until browned and cooked through, about 6 minutes per side. Drizzle pork chops with reserved syrup mixture before serving.

Stephanie Westfall, Dallas, GA

Perfect Pepper Steak

This recipe is one of my family's favorites! Sprinkle with chow mein noodles if you like a crunchy topping.

Serves 4 to 6

1-1/2 to 2 lbs. beef round steak, sliced into strips
15-oz. can diced tomatoes
1 to 2 green and/or red peppers, sliced
1 onion, chopped
4-oz. can sliced mushrooms, drained
1/4 c. salsa
cooked rice

Combine all ingredients except rice in a slow cooker. Cover and cook on low setting for 6 to 8 hours. To serve, spoon over cooked rice.

★ SLOW COOKER TO THE RESCUE! ★ Slow cookers are a super budget helper! Cheaper cuts of beef like round steak and chuck roast cook up fork-tender, juicy and flavorful. There's simply no need to purchase more expensive cuts.

Maple Pork Chops

Sheila Bane, Waynetown, IN

Creamy Fettuccine Alfredo

This has been one of my tried & true recipes for over twenty years. It's a favorite of my kids...try it and you'll agree!

Makes 6 servings

16-oz. pkg. fettuccine pasta, uncooked
1 t. salt
2/3 c. butter, softened
1-1/2 c. half-and-half, room temperature, divided
1-1/2 c. shredded Parmesan cheese
1/4 t. garlic salt
Garnish: additional shredded Parmesan cheese

Cook pasta as package directs, adding salt to cooking water. Remove pan from heat; drain pasta and return to pan. Add butter to warm pasta and mix well. Add 3/4 cup half-and-half to pasta; mix well. In a small bowl, mix together cheese and garlic salt. Add half of cheese mixture. Add remaining half-and-half and remaining cheese mixture to pasta mixture, stirring well after each addition. Garnish with additional cheese and serve immediately.

Paulette Alexander,
Newfoundland, Canada

Cream Cheese-Stuffed Chicken

One of our favorite meals! It's so easy to make and leaves everybody quite satisfied. I sometimes make it when cooking as a volunteer with elementary children at our local school.

Makes 4 servings

4 boneless, skinless chicken breasts
1/2 c. cream cheese with chives, softened
4 T. butter, softened and divided
1/2 c. brown sugar, packed
1/4 c. mustard
4 wooden toothpicks, soaked in water
Optional: cooked rice

Place each chicken breast between 2 pieces of plastic wrap. Pound to 1/4-inch thick and set aside. In a small bowl, beat cream cheese and 2 tablespoons butter to a creamy consistency. Blend in brown sugar and mustard. Divide mixture among chicken breasts; spread evenly. Fold chicken over; fasten with toothpicks. Place chicken in a single layer in a lightly greased 9"x9" baking pan. Melt remaining butter and drizzle over chicken. Bake, uncovered, at 350 degrees for 25 to 30 minutes, until chicken juices run clear. Discard toothpicks. Serve with cooked rice, if desired.

Creamy Fettuccine Alfredo

Jennifer Levy, Warners, NY

Slow-Cooker Rich Beef Stew

This recipe was given to me by my sister Karen. We both make it often for family meals, and we're also proud to serve it to company too.

Makes 6 servings

2-1/2 lbs. stew beef, cubed
10-3/4 oz. can cream of mushroom
   soup
10-3/4 oz. can French onion soup
1 c. dry red wine or beef broth
1 c. fresh mushrooms, sliced
cooked egg noodles

Combine all ingredients except noodles in a slow cooker. Stir to mix. Cover and cook on low setting for 8 to 10 hours. Serve over cooked egg noodles.

Amy James, Fayetteville, AR

Fantastic 40-Clove Chicken

You'll be amazed at how sweet and flavorful the garlic is after cooking all day. You can usually buy already-peeled garlic in the produce section.

Serves 6 to 8

4 boneless, skinless chicken breasts
2 t. salt
1 t. pepper
40 cloves garlic, peeled
3/4 c. dry white wine or chicken
   broth
1 t. dried thyme
1-1/2 t. dried rosemary
1 bay leaf
1 T. butter

Season chicken with salt and pepper; place in a slow cooker. Add garlic, wine or broth and seasonings to slow cooker. Cover and cook on low setting for 4 to 6 hours, until chicken juices run clear. Remove chicken from slow cooker and pour juices through a strainer, mashing some garlic cloves through as well. Discard bay leaf. Cook juice mixture in a saucepan over high heat until thickened, about 6 to 8 minutes. Add butter to sauce; stir until mixed. Drizzle sauce over chicken.

Slow-Cooker Rich Beef Stew

Vickie, Gooseberry Patch

Slow-Cooker Chicken Burrito Bowls with Corn Salsa

Fresh sweet corn tastes best for this salsa, but i've made it with frozen and even canned corn with good results.

Makes 4 servings

1 lb. boneless, skinless chicken
   breasts
1/2 t. chipotle chili powder
1 c. favorite salsa
2 t. olive oil
1 c. brown rice, uncooked
2 c. chicken broth or water
2 T. lime juice, divided
15-1/2 oz. can black beans, drained
   and rinsed
Garnish: 1/2 c. shredded Cheddar
   cheese, salsa, avocado slices, sour
   cream

Place chicken in a 4-quart slow cooker; sprinkle with chili powder. Spoon salsa over chicken. Cover and cook on low setting for 6 to 7 hours, or on high setting for 3 to 4 hours, until chicken is very tender. Shred chicken in slow cooker with 2 forks; keep slow cooker on low setting until ready to serve. About one hour before serving, add oil and rice to a saucepan over medium heat. Toast rice in oil for 3 to 5 minutes, stirring often. Add broth or water; bring mixture to a boil. Reduce heat to low; cover and simmer for 45 minutes. Remove from heat. Stir in lime juice; cover and let stand for 10 minutes. To serve, divide rice, chicken, black beans and Corn Salsa among 4 bowls. Garnish as desired.

Corn Salsa:

1 c. corn
1/2 c. red onion, diced
1/4 c. fresh cilantro, chopped
2 T. lime juice
salt and pepper to taste

Combine corn, onion, cilantro and lime juice in a bowl. Season with salt and pepper.

★ HOT TIP ★ Using fresh sweet corn in a recipe? When boiling corn, add sugar to the water instead of salt. Sugar will sweeten the corn while salt will make it tough.

Slow-Cooker Chicken Burrito Bowls with Corn Salsa

Banana Split Cake, Page 226

CHAPTER SIX

Blue-Ribbon Desserts

Peanut Butter Pie, Page 250

Triple Fudge Cake, Page 238

Georgia Muth, Penn Valley, CA

Cream & Cherry Pie

I cherish the nostalgic and comforting feeling I get whenever I look through my mom's recipe box. This recipe is among her treasured recipes, written in her perfect penmanship. She made this simple pie throughout my childhood and I continue to make it.

Makes 6 servings

9-inch pie crust, unbaked
1 c. whipping cream
1/2 t. almond extract
3-oz. pkg. cream cheese, softened
1/2 c. powdered sugar
21-oz. can cherry pie filling

Bake pie crust according to package directions; cool. In a deep bowl, beat whipping cream with an electric mixer on high speed until soft peaks form. Fold in extract; set aside. In another bowl, blend cream cheese with powdered sugar; fold in whipped cream mixture. Spoon mixture into baked pie crust; cover and chill for several hours. At serving time, spoon pie filling over pie; cut into wedges.

Athena Colegrove, Big Springs, TX

2-Kiss Cupcakes

Bake these for your family and you'll be guaranteed not just kisses, but several hugs, too!

Makes 2-1/2 dozen

3/4 c. butter, softened
1-2/3 c. sugar
3 eggs, beaten
1-1/2 t. vanilla extract
2 c. all-purpose flour
2/3 c. baking cocoa
1-1/4 t. baking soda
1/4 t. baking powder
1 t. salt
1-1/3 c. water
60 milk chocolate drops, divided

Beat butter, sugar, eggs and vanilla; set aside. Combine flour, cocoa, baking soda, baking powder and salt; add alternately with water to butter mixture. Fill paper-lined muffin cups half full. Place a chocolate drop in center of each. Bake at 350 degrees for 20 minutes. Let cool. Frost with Chocolate Frosting. Top each with a chocolate drop.

Chocolate Frosting:

1/4 c. butter, melted
1/2 c. baking cocoa
1/3 c. milk
1 t. vanilla extract
3-1/2 c. powdered sugar

Combine all ingredients; beat until smooth.

Cream & Cherry Pie

Catharine Fairchild, Ontario, Canada

Grandma Gare's Prize Butter Tarts

I never knew my Granma Gare, but my mom talked about her all the time and always used her recipes, all of which become instant family favorites. This is one of the best!

Makes 2 dozen

24 frozen pastry tart shells
2/3 c. butter, softened
2 c. brown sugar, packed
1/4 c. milk
1 c. raisins
2 eggs, beaten
2 t. vanilla extract

Place tart shells on a lightly greased rimmed baking sheet; set aside. In a large bowl, blend butter and brown sugar. Add milk, blending well. Add raisins, eggs and vanilla, combine thoroughly. Spoon mixture into tart shells, filling 3/4 full. Bake at 375 degrees for 15 to 18 minutes, until golden. Cool tarts completely before removing from pan.

Henry Burnley, Ankeny, IA

Brownie Buttons

These little bits of chocolate, caramel and peanut butter will be the sweet goodie they ask for again and again.

Makes 20

16-oz. pkg. refrigerated mini brownie bites dough
11-oz. pkg. assorted mini peanut butter cup candies and chocolate-coated caramels

Spray mini muffin cups with non-stick vegetable spray. Spoon brownie dough evenly into each cup, filling almost full. Bake at 350 degrees for 19 to 20 minutes. Cool in pans 3 to 4 minutes; gently press a candy into each baked brownie until top of candy is level with top of brownie. Cool 10 minutes in pans. Gently twist each brownie to remove from pan. Cool on a wire rack

Grandma Gare's Prize Butter Tarts

Cindy Jamieson, Ontario, Canada

Apple Tarts

My mom would often make these yummy tarts during the cooler fall days. I've made a few changes, to add wonderful warmth to them. They are spectacular served with a scoop of ice cream, a drizzle of caramel sauce and a sprinkle of toasted almonds.

Makes 4 tarts

4 Nova Spy or Granny Smith
  apples, peeled, cored and chopped
1/3 c. brown sugar, packed
1/4 c. all-purpose flour
1/4 t. cinnamon
1/8 t. nutmeg
1/8 t. ground cloves
1/4 t. lemon zest
1/2 t. lemon juice
1/2 t. vanilla extract
2 9-inch pie crusts, unbaked
1/4 c. milk, divided
2 T. sugar, divided
Garnish: vanilla ice cream,
  caramel sauce, toasted sliced
  almonds

In a saucepan, combine apples, brown sugar, flour, spices, lemon zest, lemon juice and vanilla. Cook over medium-low heat, stirring occasionally, until mixture comes to a boil. Reduce heat to low; simmer until apples are just tender. Cool slightly. Meanwhile, roll out one pie crust on a floured surface, 1/8-inch thick. Cut out 4 dough circles, each 4 inches in diameter; repeat with remaining crusts. Press bottom crust into 4" tart pan. Spoon 1/2 cup filling into filled pan. Lay second circle on top of the filling. Wet edges with a bit of milk and seal by pressing the edges together in a fluted edge. Cut several small slits in top of tart. Brush tarts with milk and lightly sprinkle with sugar. Place filled tart pans on ungreased baking sheets. Bake at 375 degrees for 25 to 30 minutes, until golden. Serve warm, garnish as desired.

★ THE RIGHT TIMING ★ To avoid overbaking, set your timer for 3 minutes fewer than the allotted time. Ovens can vary in temperature, so checking for doneness a little early will ensure excellent baked goods every time.

Apple Tarts

Charlotte Smith, Tyrone, PA

Banana Split Cake

Oh my, this is so yummy! Whenever I take this cake to a potluck, the pan comes home empty.

Makes 10 servings

2 c. graham cracker crumbs
6 T. butter, melted
2 pasteurized eggs, beaten
2 c. powdered sugar
1/4 c. margarine, softened
3 firm bananas, sliced
Optional: 1/2 c. lemon-lime soda
20-oz. can crushed pineapple, well
    drained
8-oz. container frozen whipped
    topping, thawed
6-oz. jar maraschino cherries,
    drained and chopped
1/2 c. chopped walnuts

In a bowl, mix together cracker crumbs and butter. Press firmly into the bottom of a 13"x9" baking pan; set aside. In another bowl, beat together eggs, powdered sugar and margarine for 5 minutes, or until smooth; spread over crumb mixture. If desired, dip banana slices into soda to prevent browning; drain. Layer banana slices over powdered sugar mixture; top with pineapple. Spread whipped topping over pineapple. Garnish with cherries; sprinkle with walnuts. Cover and refrigerate for one hour before serving. Cut into squares.

Jo Ann, Gooseberry Patch

Prize-Winning Funnel Cakes

The kid in all of us loves the powdered sugar topping! Or treat yourself to a big dollop of fruit pie filling.

Makes about 4 servings

2 c. all-purpose flour
1 T. sugar
1 t. baking powder
1/4 t. salt
2 eggs, beaten
1-1/4 c. milk
oil for deep frying
Garnish: powdered sugar
Optional: apple, cherry or blueberry
    pie filling

Sift together flour, sugar, baking powder and salt into a deep bowl. Make a well in the center; add eggs and enough milk to make a thin batter. Mix well. In a cast-iron skillet, heat 2 inches oil to 375 degrees. With a fingertip over end of funnel, drop batter by 1/2 cupfuls into a funnel over hot oil, one at a time, swirling funnel as batter is released. Cook until golden, about 2 minutes per side. Drain on paper towels. Sprinkle with powdered sugar; top with pie filling, if desired. Serve immediately.

Banana Split Cake

Teresa Verell, Roanoke, VA

Favorite Pecan Pie Cobbler

This recipe has been in the Verell family for over 25 years. It is always requested for our July 4th cookout. It is easy and delicious.

Makes 16 servings

1/2 c. butter, melted
1 c. self-rising flour
1-2/3 c. sugar, divided
1 c. whole milk
1/2 c. butter, softened
3 eggs, lightly beaten
1 c. dark corn syrup
1 c. chopped pecans

Pour melted butter into a 13"x9" baking pan; set aside. In a bowl, mix flour, one cup sugar and milk; spoon over butter in pan. In another bowl, mix together softened butter, remaining sugar, eggs, corn syrup and pecans; pour over crust mixture in pan. Do not stir. Bake at 350 degrees for 35 to 40 minutes, until set. Cool; cut into squares.

Jo Ann, Gooseberry Paatch

Bananas Foster

Guests will flip over this decadent slow-cooker dessert!

Makes 4 servings

1/2 c. butter, melted
1/4 c. brown sugar, packed
6 bananas, cut into 1-inch slices
1/4 c. rum or 1/4 t. rum extract
Garnish: vanilla ice cream

Stir together butter, brown sugar, bananas and rum or extract in a slow cooker. Cover and cook on low setting for one hour. Use a slotted spoon to place bananas into serving dishes. Top with a scoop of ice cream and drizzle with sauce from the slow cooker.

★ DRIZZLE THIS! ★ Whip up a tasty cinnamon glaze to drizzle over your favorite dessert or quick bread. Mix 1/2 cup powdered sugar and 1/4 teaspoon cinnamon. Add one teaspoon light corn syrup; stir in apple juice, one tablespoon at a time, until a drizzling consistency is reached.

Favorite Pecan Pie Cobbler

Brenda Smith, Delaware, OH

Caramel-Glazed Apple Cake

This made-from-scratch cake with its luscious glaze is irresistible! It's also easy to tote to holiday get-togethers or potlucks in its baking pan.

Makes 16 servings

1-1/2 c. butter, softened
1 c. sugar
1 c. brown sugar, packed
3 eggs
3 c. all-purpose flour
2 t. cinnamon
1 t. baking soda
1/2 t. nutmeg
1/2 t. salt
5 Granny Smith apples, cored,
    peeled and diced
1-1/4 c. chopped pecans
2-1/4 t. vanilla extract

In a large bowl, beat butter and sugars with an electric mixer at medium-high speed, until light and fluffy. Add eggs, one at a time, beating after each addition. In a separate bowl, combine flour, cinnamon, baking soda, nutmeg and salt. Gradually add flour mixture to butter mixture with a wooden spoon to form a very thick batter. Stir in remaining ingredients. Pour batter into a greased and floured 13"x9" baking pan. Bake at 325 degrees for 50 to 60 minutes, until a toothpick inserted in center comes out clean. Cool cake in pan on a wire rack for at least 10 minutes. Poke holes all over surface of cake with a fork. Pour warm Caramel Glaze over cake. Serve warm or cooled.

Caramel Glaze:

1/4 c. butter
1/4 c. sugar
1/4 c. brown sugar, packed
1/8 t. salt
1/2 c. whipping cream

Melt butter in a saucepan over medium-low heat. Add sugars and salt. Cook, stirring frequently, for 2 minutes. Stir in cream and bring to a boil. Cook, stirring constantly, for 2 minutes.

★ HANDY TIP ★ A great way to keep brown sugar from hardening is to drop a slice of fresh apple in the bag...it absorbs extra moisture.

Caramel Glazed Apple Cake

Tina Wright, Atlanta, GA

Pecan Cheesecake Pie

For a quick variation, try walnut halves in place of pecans.

Makes 8 servings

9-inch refrigerated pie crust
8-oz. pkg. cream cheese, softened
4 eggs, divided
3/4 c. sugar, divided
2 t. vanilla extract, divided
1/4 t. salt
1-1/4 c. chopped pecans
1 c. light corn syrup

Fit pie crust into a 9" pie plate according to package directions. Fold edges under and crimp; set aside. Beat cream cheese, one egg, 1/2 cup sugar, one teaspoon vanilla and salt with an electric mixer at medium speed until smooth. Pour cream cheese mixture into pie crust; sprinkle evenly with chopped pecans. Whisk together corn syrup and remaining eggs, sugar and vanilla; pour mixture over pecans. Place pie on a baking sheet. Bake at 350 degrees on lowest oven rack 50 to 55 minutes, until pie is set. Cool on a wire rack one hour or until completely cool. Serve immediately or cover and chill up to 2 days.

Nina Jones, Springfield, OH

Little Cheesecakes

I started making this recipe when I was a teenager...now it's a favorite of my teenage son and his friends.

Makes 2 dozen

1 c. graham cracker crumbs
1 c. sugar, divided
1/4 c. butter, melted
2 8-oz. pkgs. cream cheese, softened
2 eggs, beaten
1 t. vanilla extract
14-1/2 oz. can cherry pie filling

Place mini paper liners into 24 mini muffin cups. In a bowl, combine cracker crumbs, 1/4 cup sugar and butter. Press about 2 teaspoons of mixture into the bottom of each liner. In a bowl, beat cream cheese and remaining sugar together. Add eggs and vanilla; mix well. Evenly spoon cheese mixture over crusts. Bake at 350 degrees for 15 minutes, or until set. Cool. Top with cherry pie filling.

Pecan Cheesecake Pie

Dianna Oakland, Titusville, FL

Dianna's Best Tiramisu

I have tried many versions of this dessert, and this one is by far the best. Everyone always asks for seconds... and the recipe!

Serves 16 to 24

1 c. brewed coffee, cooled
1/2 c. plus 1 T. sugar, divided
2 8-oz. pkgs. cream cheese, softened
2 T. almond-flavored liqueur or 1/4 to 1/2 t. almond extract
12-oz. container frozen whipped topping, thawed
16-oz. pound cake, cut into 30 slices
1 T. baking cocoa

Combine coffee and one tablespoon sugar in a medium bowl; set aside. In a bowl, beat cream cheese with an electric mixer at medium speed, until fluffy. Add remaining sugar and almond liqueur or extract. Gently fold in whipped topping and set aside. Layer 10 cake slices on the bottom of an ungreased 13"x9" baking pan. Brush one-third of coffee mixture over cake slices with a pastry brush. Top with one-third of cream cheese mixture. Repeat 2 more times to create 3 layers. Sprinkle cocoa over top and chill overnight.

Mary Nguyen, Oklahoma City, OK

Millionaire Brownies

These are the very best brownies I've ever had...they're a big hit with my family too!

Makes 2 dozen

18-1/4 oz. pkg. chocolate fudge cake mix
1 c. evaporated milk, divided
3/4 c. butter, softened
14-oz. pkg. caramels, unwrapped
1-1/2 c. semi-sweet chocolate chips
1-1/2 c. chopped pecans

In a large bowl, combine dry cake mix, 2/3 cup evaporated milk and butter; stir until moistened. Spread half of batter in a greased 13"x9" baking pan. Bake at 350 degrees for 8 minutes; cool. Melt caramels with remaining milk in a small saucepan over low heat, stirring constantly. Sprinkle brownies with chocolate chips; drizzle with caramel mixture. Top with pecans. Spread remaining batter over top. Bake at 350 degrees for 18 to 20 minutes. Cool completely before cutting.

Dianna's Best Tiramisu

Kelly Marcum, Rock Falls, IL

Grandma's Banana Cupcakes

My grandma used to make these often...they were so yummy! I like to drizzle a little caramel sauce over the tops to make them extra special.

Makes 1-1/2 to 2 dozen

1/2 c. butter, softened
1-3/4 c. sugar
2 eggs
2 c. all-purpose flour
1 t. baking powder
1 t. baking soda
1/4 t. salt
1 c. buttermilk
2 bananas, mashed
1 t. vanilla extract
Optional: 24 toasted pecan
  halves, sliced banana

In a large bowl, beat butter and sugar with an electric mixer at medium speed, until light and fluffy. Add eggs, one at a time, beating after each addition. In a separate bowl, combine flour, baking powder, baking soda and salt; add to batter alternately with buttermilk, beginning and ending with flour mixture. Beat at low speed after each addition until blended. Stir in bananas and vanilla. Fill paper-lined muffin cups 1/2 full. Bake at 350 degrees for 18 to 25 minutes, until a toothpick inserted in center comes out clean. Remove to wire racks to cool completely; frost with Cream Cheese Frosting. Store frosted cupcakes in an airtight container in refrigerator. Garnish each cupcake with a pecan half and banana slice just before serving, if desired.

Cream Cheese Frosting:

8-oz. pkg. cream cheese, softened
1/2 c. butter, softened
1 t. vanilla extract
1/8 t. salt
16-oz. pkg. powdered sugar

In a large bowl, beat cream cheese, butter, vanilla and salt with an electric mixer at medium speed, until creamy. Gradually add powdered sugar, beating until fluffy.

★ KITCHEN HELPER! ★ A potato masher is useful for lots more than potatoes! Mash apples for applesauce and bananas for breads and cakes. It's so easy!

Grandma's Banana Cupcakes

Tanya Leach, Adamstown, PA

Triple Fudge Cake

I get requests for this cake all the time, and nothing could be easier to make!

Makes 12 servings

3.4-oz. pkg. cook & serve
   chocolate pudding mix
18-1/4 oz. pkg. chocolate cake mix
12-oz. pkg. semi-sweet
   chocolate chips
Optional: vanilla ice cream

Prepare pudding according to package directions; stir in cake mix. Spread in a greased 13"x9" baking pan; sprinkle with chocolate chips. Bake at 350 degrees for 35 minutes; cool. Serve with vanilla ice cream, if desired.

Jacklyn Akey, Merrill, WI

Chocolaty Chewy Brownies

You'll love these chewy little squares of chocolate!

Makes about 2 dozen

1 c. butter, softened
2 c. sugar
4 eggs, beaten
1 c. all-purpose flour
4 1-oz. sqs. unsweetened baking
   chocolate, melted
1 c. chopped walnuts
Optional: powdered sugar

In a bowl, beat butter and sugar with an electric mixer on medium speed, until creamy. Beat in eggs, mixing well. Stir in remaining ingredients. Pour into a greased and floured 13"x9" baking pan. Bake at 350 degrees for 30 minutes. Cool. Dust with powdered sugar if desired. Cut into squares.

Triple Fudge Cake

Kierstan Abrams, Los Angeles, CA

Blue-Ribbon Banana Cake

Garnish with a dollop of whipped cream and a dusting of cinnamon... yummy!

Serves 12 to 16

1/2 c. shortening
1/4 c. plus 2 T. butter, softened and divided
2 c. sugar, divided
2 eggs
1 c. bananas, mashed
1 c. chopped pecans, divided
2 c. cake flour
1 t. baking soda
1 t. baking powder
3/4 t. salt, divided
2 t. vanilla extract, divided
1/2 c. buttermilk
1/4 c. sweetened flaked coconut
1/2 c. all-purpose flour
1/2 c. half-and-half
Garnish: sweetened flaked coconut

Combine shortening, 1/4 cup butter and 1-1/2 cups sugar in a large bowl; beat with an electric mixer at medium speed until fluffy. Add eggs and bananas; beat 2 minutes. Stir in 1/2 cup pecans. Sift together cake flour, baking soda, baking powder and 1/2 teaspoon salt; add to shortening mixture. Add one teaspoon vanilla and buttermilk; beat 2 minutes.

Divide batter equally between 2 greased and floured 9" round cake pans; sprinkle batter with coconut. Bake at 350 degrees for 25 to 30 minutes. Cool cakes 10 minutes before removing from pans. Combine flour, half-and-half and remaining sugar and butter in a saucepan over medium heat; cook until thickened, whisking frequently. Add remaining nuts, salt and vanilla, stirring well; cool. Place first cake, coconut-side down, on a serving platter; spread thickened sugar mixture over top. Place second layer, coconut-side up, over first cake. Swirl on Snow White Frosting, leaving center of cake unfrosted so coconut can be seen. Garnish with additional sweetened flaked coconut.

Snow White Frosting:

1 egg white
1/4 c. shortening
1/4 c. butter, softened
1/4 t. almond extract
1/2 t. vanilla extract
2 c. powdered sugar

Combine egg white, shortening, butter and extracts in a large bowl; blend well. Gradually add powdered sugar, beating until fluffy if desired.

Blue-Ribbon Banana Cake

Marilyn Morel, Keene, NH

Hello Dolly Bars

My sister began making these in the late 1970s, and I make them every time I need a little pick-me-up. My sister is no longer with us, but these wonderful treats hold some very special memories for me, which I have passed down to my children and now my grandson.

Serves 12 to 16

1/2 c. margarine, melted
1 c. graham cracker crumbs
1 c. sweetened flaked coconut
6-oz. pkg. semi-sweet chocolate
    chips
6-oz. pkg. butterscotch chips
14-oz. can sweetened condensed
    milk
1 c. chopped pecans

Combine margarine and graham cracker crumbs in a bowl and mix well; press into a lightly greased 9"x9" baking pan. Top with layers of coconut, chocolate chips and butterscotch chips. Pour condensed milk over top; sprinkle with pecans. Bake at 350 degrees for 25 to 30 minutes. Cool; cut into bars.

Sarah Muennix, Flint, MI

Prize-Winning Almond Bundt Cake

I entered this Bundt cake into a baking contest at our local food store. It took home second place...and the bakery adopted this recipe to place alongside their other "gourmet" cakes!

Makes 12 servings

2-1/2 c. sugar
2 eggs, beaten
2-1/2 t. almond extract
1-1/3 c. milk
1 c. butter, softened
2-1/2 c. all-purpose flour
1 t. baking powder
1/4 t. cinnamon
Garnish: chopped almonds,
    raw sugar

In a bowl, beat together sugar, eggs, extract, milk and butter. Gradually add flour, baking powder and cinnamon; beat well. Sprinkle almonds and raw sugar in the bottom of a greased Bundt® pan; pour batter over almonds and sugar. Bake at 350 degrees for 50 minutes, or until a toothpick tests clean. Cool cake in pan for 15 to 20 minutes. Turn out onto a wire rack. Serve warm or cooled.

Hello Dolly Bars

Lauren Williams, Kewanee, MO

Coconut Cream Pie

I have such fond memories of when my dad's family would all get together to eat at a local restaurant. Their coconut cream pie was one of my favorites! This is my own version.

Makes 10 servings

2 c. milk
1/3 c. sugar
1/4 c. cornstarch
1/4 t. salt
3 egg yolks, beaten
1-1/2 c. sweetened flaked coconut, divided
2 T. butter, softened
1/2 t. vanilla extract
9-inch pie crust, baked

Combine milk, sugar, cornstarch and salt in a large saucepan; cook over medium heat until thickened, stirring constantly. Remove from heat. Place egg yolks in a small bowl. Stir a small amount of hot milk mixture into egg yolks. Pour yolk mixture back into saucepan; simmer gently for 2 minutes. Stir in one cup coconut, butter and vanilla. Pour into crust. Spread Meringue over hot pie filling; seal to edges. Sprinkle with remaining coconut. Bake at 350 degrees for 12 minutes, or until golden.

Meringue:

4 egg whites
7-oz. jar marshmallow creme

Beat egg whites in a bowl with an electric mixer at high speed until stiff peaks form. Add marshmallow creme; beat for 2 minutes, or until well blended.

★ DRESS IT UP! ★ Dress up a mouthwatering coconut pie by placing it on an old-fashioned pedestal plate. Elegance in a jiffy!

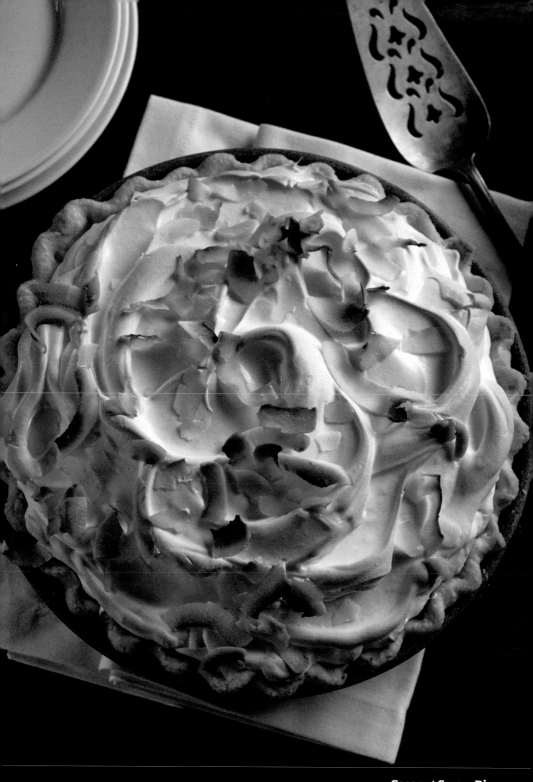

Coconut Cream Pie

Linda Jancik, Lakewood, OH

Creamsicles

Fresh orange juice makes these creamy frozen treats taste so much better than store-bought.

Makes one dozen

1 pt. vanilla ice cream or ice milk, softened
6-oz. can frozen orange juice concentrate, thawed
1/4 c. honey
1-1/2 c. fat-free milk
12 craft sticks

Combine ice cream or ice milk, orange juice concentrate and honey in a large bowl; mix well. Gradually beat in fat-free milk and pour into 12 small wax paper cups or an ice cube tray. Insert sticks into paper cups or ice cube trays when partially frozen; freeze until solid.

Judy Borecky, Escondido, CA

Judy's Prize-Winning Toasted Pecan Cake

This local winner was featured on the front page of the San Diego newspaper!

Makes 12 servings

2 c. chopped pecans
1-1/4 c. butter, softened and divided
3 c. all-purpose flour
2 t. baking powder
1/2 t. salt
2 c. sugar
4 eggs, beaten
1 c. milk
2 t. vanilla extract

Combine pecans and 1/4 cup butter; spread on a baking sheet. Bake at 350 degrees for 15 minutes, stirring often; cool. Mix flour, baking powder and salt. In a separate bowl, blend remaining butter and sugar; stir in eggs. Add flour mixture to butter mixture alternately with milk, beating well. Stir in vanilla and 1-1/3 cups pecans. Pour into 3 greased and floured 8" round cake pans. Bake at 350 degrees for 20 to 25 minutes, until cake tests done. Cool before frosting.

Frosting:

1/4 c. butter, softened
16-oz. pkg. powdered sugar
1 t. vanilla extract
4 to 6 T. evaporated milk
2/3 c. reserved toasted pecans

Beat all ingredients except pecans until smooth. Stir in pecans.

Creamsicles

Cynthia Dodge, Layton, UT

Chocolate-Orange Zucchini Cake

You will beg your neighbors to leave zucchini on your doorstep after eating this moist, rich cake! It tastes like your favorite orange-shaped chocolate candy...yum!

Makes 12 servings

1/2 c. plus 2 T. baking cocoa, divided
2-1/2 c. plus 2 T. all-purpose flour, divided
1/2 c. butter
2 c. sugar
3 eggs
2 t. vanilla extract
zest of 1 orange
1/2 c. milk
3 T. canola oil
3 c. zucchini, peeled and shredded
2-1/2 t. baking powder
1-1/2 t. baking soda
1/2 t. salt
1/2 t. cinnamon
Garnish: baking cocoa

Spray a 10-inch Bundt® pan with non-stick vegetable spray. Mix 2 tablespoons cocoa with 2 tablespoons flour. Coat interior of pan with mixture; shake out any extra and set aside pan. In a large bowl, beat butter and sugar with an electric mixer on medium speed. Add eggs, one at a time, beating well after each addition. Stir in vanilla, orange zest and milk. In a separate bowl, combine remaining cocoa and oil; mix thoroughly. Add cocoa mixture to butter mixture; stir well. Fold in zucchini. Add remaining flour and other ingredients. Beat on low speed until well blended. Pour into prepared pan. Bake at 350 degrees for about one hour, until a wooden toothpick tests clean. Cool in pan for 10 minutes; remove from pan to a cake plate. Cool completely. Dust top of cake with baking cocoa.

★ BAKING COCOA ★ Use for baking cakes, brownies, making frrostings and hot chocolate. Extra bonus...baking cocoa is naturally low in fat and cholesterol-free. For an extra-special treat, try sprinkling sweetened baking cocoa on top of vanilla ice cream or yogurt. Yum!

Chocolate-Orange Zucchini Cake

Carol Nebzydoski, Pleasant Mount, PA

Peanut Butter Pie

My kids have always loved this creamy, peanut buttery pie. My 21-year-old son even called from Texas while he was in the army and asked for the recipe so he could make it for a small gathering of friends before they left for Iraq.

Makes 8 servings

1/2 c. sugar
1/2 c. creamy or crunchy
   peanut butter
3-oz. pkg. cream cheese,
   softened
12-oz. container frozen whipped
   topping, thawed
9-inch graham cracker crust
Optional: additional whipped
   cream, chopped peanuts

Combine sugar, peanut butter and cream cheese in a large bowl; stir until well blended. Fold in whipped topping. Spoon mixture into pie crust. Cover and chill at least 2 hours before serving. Top with additional whipped cream and chopped peanuts, if desired.

Mary Patenaude, Griswold, CT

Root Beer Float Cake

This cake is so easy to make. And it tastes just like a root beer float!

Makes 24 servings

18-1/2 oz. pkg. white cake mix
2-1/4 c. root beer, chilled and divided
1/4 c. oil
2 eggs, beaten
1 env. whipped topping mix

In a large bowl, combine dry cake mix, 1-1/4 cups root beer, oil and eggs; beat until well blended. Pour into a greased 13"x9" baking pan. Bake at 350 degrees for 30 to 35 minutes; cool completely. In a medium bowl, with an electric mixer on high speed, beat whipped topping mix and remaining root beer until soft peaks form; frost cake.

★ HANDY TIP ★ Need to soften cream cheese in a hurry? Simply place an unwrapped 8-ounce block on a plate and microwave for about a minute at 50% power.

Peanut Butter Pie

Index

Appetizers

3-Cheese Artichoke Bites, p.44
Almond Toffee Popcorn, p.12
Avocado Feta Dip, p.44
Bacon-Sausage Rye Crisps, p.18
Bacon-Wrapped Scallops, p.34
Best Fry Batter, p.30
Best Mexican Dip Ever, p.10
Best-Ever Cheese Spread, p.36
Best-Ever Garlic Cheese Spread, p.16
BLT Bites, p.40
Cheesesteak Egg Rolls, p.26
Cheesy Spinach-Stuffed Mushrooms, p.24
Cheesy Tuna Melts, p.22
Chinese Chicken Wings, p.30
Chip Chicken Lollipops, p.24
Confetti Cheesecake, p.42
Corn Dog Mini Muffins, p.22
Crunchy Artichoke Fries, p.8
Easy Gumbo Meatballs, p.18
Fried Dill Pickles, p.8
Herb-Seasoned Spinach Puffs, p.28
Incredible Mini Burger Bites, p.38
Jalapeño Cheddar Balls, p.14
Market Veggie Triangles, p.40
Pepperoni Pizza Braid, p.20
Savory Bacon Bites, p.36
Sesame Chicken Tea Sandwiches, p.16
Spicy Hummus, p.32
Spicy Ranch Party Pretzels, p.12
Spiedini, p.28
Tangy Radish Bites, p.34
Texas Caviar, p.32
Waffle Fry Nachos, p.10

Breads

Bacon-Corn Muffins, p.106
Best-Ever Southern Cornbread, p.110
Blueberry Scones, p.126
Cheddar-Chive Muffins, p.118
Creamy Cinnamon Rolls, p.86
Delicious Quick Rolls, p.120
Dutch Baby with Spiced Fruit, p.54
Fluffy Whole-Wheat Biscuits, p.114
Garlic-Cheddar Beer Biscuits, p.106
Grandma's Best Cinnamon-Sugar Bread, p.98
Herbed Cheese Focaccia, p.114
Italian Bread, p.110
Lemon Tea Bread, p.118
Lemon-Rosemary Zucchini Bread, p.94
Mother's Pull-Apart Cheese Bread, p.120
Orange Coffee Rolls, p.82
Overnight Caramel Pecan Rolls, p.86
Peanut Butter Muffins, p.80
Sweet Potato Cornbread, p.94

Breakfasts

Apple-Sausage Pancakes, p.60
Baked Shrimp & Grits, p.84
Best-Ever Breakfast Bars, p.76